My eLab | Efficient teaching, effective learning

My eLab is the interactive environment that gives you access to self-graded exercises and additional study resources related to your textbook. Be sure to register for **My eLab** to ensure your success!

TO REGISTER

❶ Go to **http://mybookshelf.pearsonerpi.com**

❷ Click on "NOT REGISTERED YET?" and follow the instructions. When asked for your access code, please type the code provided underneath the blue sticker.

❸ To access **My eLab** at any time, go to http://mybookshelf.pearsonerpi.com. **Bookmark this page for quicker access.**

Access to My eLab is valid for 12 months from the date of registration.

WARNING! This book CANNOT BE RETURNED if the access code has been uncovered.

Note: Once you have registered, you will need to join your online class. Ask your teacher to provide you with the class ID.

TEACHER Access Code

To obtain an access code for My eLab, please contact your Pearson ELT consultant.

1 800 263-3678, ext.2
pearsonerpi.com/help

W135563 (A55850)

DR. KEN BEATTY

leap 2

LISTENING AND SPEAKING **Intermediate**

Learning English for Academic Purposes

PEARSON

Managing Editor
Sharnee Chait

Project Editor
Linda Barton

Proofreader
Mairi MacKinnon

Coordinator, Rights and Permissions
Pierre Richard Bernier

Text Rights and Permissions
Rachel Irwin

Art Director
Hélène Cousineau

Graphic Design Coordinator
Lyse LeBlanc

Book and Cover Design
Frédérique Bouvier

Book Layout
Interscript

The publisher thanks the following people for their helpful
comments and suggestions:

Jerry Block, Fraser International College

Michelle Duhaney, Seneca College

Linda Feuer, University of Manitoba

Carleen Gruntman, Laval University

Brianna Hilman, University of Calgary

Kristibeth Kelly Delgado, Fanshawe College

Marcia Kim, University of Calgary

Izabella Kojic-Sabo, University of Windsor

Jennifer MacDonald, Dalhousie University

Tiffany MacDonald, East Coast School of Languages, Halifax

Karen Rauser, University of British Columbia

Cyndy Reimer, Douglas College

Darren Wilson, Bow Valley College

Dedication

To Margaret Atwood and all others who give reason to celebrate
language.

Audio and Video Text Credits

Chapter 1, p. 5 "Ben Silbermann at Startup School" © Y Combinator.
p. 18 "Hack to Start: Heather Payne" © Hack to Start (www.hacktostart.com).

Chapter 2, p. 33 "Students Create Their Own Dream Jobs" © Canadian
Broadcasting Corporation. p. 38 "Crowdworkers" © Canadian Broadcasting
Corporation.

Chapter 3, p. 48 "Autonomous Cars and the Future of Cities" © Canadian
Broadcasting Corporation. p. 53 "Plugging in: The Future of Electric Cars"
© Canadian Broadcasting Corporation.

Chapter 4, p. 70 "Better Brains" © The New York Academy of Sciences.
p. 75 "Ted Cadsby—Interview with Amanda Lang" © Canadian Broadcasting
Corporation.

Chapter 5, p. 92 "3D Printing" © Canadian Broadcasting Corporation.
p. 97 "The Revolution Will Be Extruded" © Canadian Broadcasting
Corporation.

Chapter 6, p. 114 "Activity Trackers and Apps" © Canadian Broadcasting
Corporation. p. 124 "Mapping Your Chromosomes" © Canadian Broadcasting
Corporation.

Chapter 7, p. 135 "Gamification" © Canadian Broadcasting Corporation.
p. 141 "Khan Academy" © Canadian Broadcasting Corporation.

Chapter 8, p. 156 "Technocreep" © Canadian Broadcasting Corporation.
p. 167 "Restoring Harmony after Murder" © Brent Stafford Executive
Producer, Shaky Egg Communications.

INTRODUCTION

Listening and speaking are our first skills, the ones we learn before we can read or write. Yet listening, in particular, is neglected in post-secondary education. This is in part because listening cannot be directly observed; although we all hear, we do not necessarily listen. *LEAP Intermediate: Listening and Speaking* recognizes this and looks for ways to prepare students to listen and speak in the world of academic discourse.

Academic discourse has many conventions with which students are often unfamiliar. These include both listening to lectures, debates and discussions, and taking notes on them, effectively and efficiently. Students then need the discussion, debate and presentation strategies that help them engage in their learning.

The bulk of the twenty-four audio and video excerpts in *LEAP Intermediate: Listening and Speaking* are authentic and feature a broad range of academic disciplines including business, computing, education, engineering, ethics, medicine and psychology. Genres focus on different styles including debates, interviews, lectures, podcasts and speeches. Students develop speaking skills in the same genres to explore how to communicate new ideas.

Throughout, graphic organizers help students develop their comprehension and critical thinking skills. In terms of assessment, assignments allow students to demonstrate what they have learned in creative and individual ways. Developing competencies is part of the Focus on Listening, Speaking and Grammar, as well as Academic Survival Skill, sections. Academic survival skills recognize that success in learning is based on developing skills such as body language, intonation, rhythm and stress patterns, group work and proper citation and referencing. Beyond the book, extensive online resources address the needs of less able students who are willing to commit time to become better as well as more able students who want to be the best.

A great deal of effort has gone into making *LEAP Intermediate: Listening and Speaking* an ideal resource, including the input of teachers across Canada and around the world where earlier versions of *LEAP* are used. Many have contributed ideas that helped make this a better resource.

ACKNOWLEDGEMENTS

Editors help writers continuously improve their craft and the talented Sharnee Chait and Linda Barton have been a constant inspiration. I thank my graduate students and colleagues at Anaheim University for ongoing discussions and ideas about teaching and learning, listening and speaking. I particularly thank my colleague, friend, occasional co-author and Ph.D. advisor David Nunan for his generous mentorship.

The fingerprints of many teachers too numerous to name are found on these pages. To those who e-mailed me privately or spoke on issues with me at conferences, thank you. I also appreciate the thoughtful contributions of those dedicated professionals who helped through conversations, focus groups, interviews, questionnaires and chapter reviews: Erica Ferrer Ariza and staff at Universidad del Norte, Barranquilla, Colombia and Alevtina Telnova, Moscow Institute of Physics and Technology, Russia.

Dr. Ken Beatty, Bowen Island, Canada

HIGHLIGHTS

Gearing Up stimulates students' interest by tapping into their prior knowledge.

The **overview** outlines the chapter objectives and features.

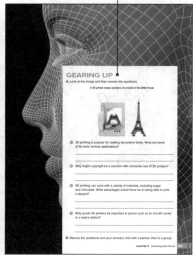

Vocabulary Build sections (three per chapter) aid comprehension and build awareness of key vocabulary on the Academic Word List.

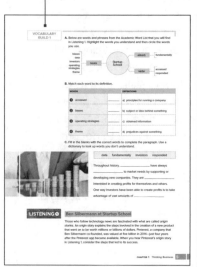

The **listenings**, including one video per chapter, vary in types including debates, interviews, lectures, podcasts and speeches.

Before You Listen activities elicit students' prior knowledge of a subject and stimulate interest.

Focus on Listening develops specific skills students need to fully understand the content and structure of academic texts. Each chapter has a **Pronunciation** and a **Develop Your Vocabulary** sidebar that provide hints and tips to students.

While You Listen activities engage students in a variety of active listening strategies, including taking notes.

After You Listen activities give students an opportunity to reflect on personal or larger issues related to what they have heard.

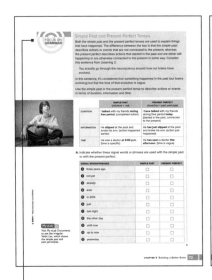

Focus on Speaking develops the skills students need to effectively discuss issues using academic English.

Focus on Grammar reviews important grammar features that students can apply when listening to and speaking about academic English.

The **Warm-Up Assignment** prepares students for the Final Assignment. Each chapter focuses on a different task.

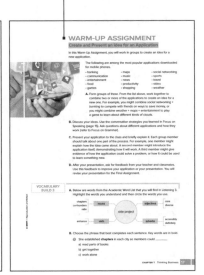

Academic Survival Skill helps students develop essential skills for academic coursework.

The **Final Assignment** synthesizes the chapter content and theme in an in-depth speaking task. Each chapter focuses on a different type of assignment.

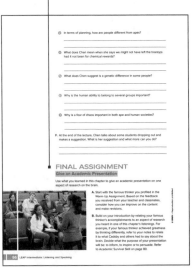

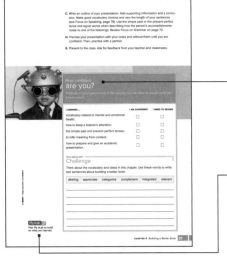

How confident are you? and **Vocabulary Challenge** allow students to reflect on their learning, decide what they need to review and use new vocabulary. **References to My eLab** point students toward additional content, practice and support.

SCOPE AND SEQUENCE

CHAPTER	LISTENING	SPEAKING
CHAPTER 1 **THINKING BUSINESS** SUBJECT AREAS: business, computing, technology	• Listening for the main idea	• Managing a conversation
CHAPTER 2 **A NEW WORLD OF WORK** SUBJECT AREAS: business, education, technology	• Using active listening strategies	• Using intonation and stress
CHAPTER 3 **PEOPLE IN MOTION** SUBJECT AREAS: engineering, transportation, urban planning	• Listening for a purpose	• Learning interviewing skills
CHAPTER 4 **BUILDING A BETTER BRAIN** SUBJECT AREAS: biology, neuroscience, psychology	• Inferring meaning from context	• Keeping a listener's attention
CHAPTER 5 **INVENTING THE FUTURE** SUBJECT AREAS: computing, engineering	• Building schema	• Using register and tone
CHAPTER 6 **ENGINEERING THE FUTURE** SUBJECT AREAS: engineering, genetics, medicine	• Predicting and inferring ideas	• Speaking with aids
CHAPTER 7 **NEW WAYS TO LEARN** SUBJECT AREAS: business, computing, education	• Listening for rhythm	• Enhancing your message with non-verbal communication
CHAPTER 8 **FINDING JUSTICE** SUBJECT AREAS: history, law, technology	• Distinguishing fact from opinion	• Constructing an argument

GRAMMAR	ACADEMIC SURVIVAL SKILL	ASSIGNMENTS
• Yes/no questions and information questions	• Taking notes and using graphic organizers	• Creating and presenting an idea for an application • Giving a presentation and taking notes
• Comparative and superlative form	• Giving a compare and contrast presentation • Citing sources and referencing	• Describing the perfect job • Giving a compare and contrast presentation
• Indirect and tag questions	• Creating survey questions	• Conducting an oral survey • Preparing and presenting an oral survey
• Simple past and present perfect tenses	• Giving academic presentations	• Introducing a famous brain • Giving an academic presentation
• Sentence types	• Developing teamwork skills	• Developing product proposals • Conducting a meeting to discuss proposals
• Conditional sentences	• Paraphrasing and summarizing	• Summarizing an interview • Participating in a group discussion
• Gerunds and infinitives	• Starting a discussion with a thesis statement	• Giving a process presentation • Taking part in an academic discussion
• Modals that express possibility	• Using debating strategies	• Giving a persuasive presentation • Participating in a debate

TABLE OF CONTENTS

CHAPTER 1

Thinking Business

A hundred years ago, starting a large business involved much more than a good idea. You would build a factory and hire hundreds of employees. The employees would work together to make products and then ship them to shops by truck, train or boat. But many of today's wealthiest innovators have created businesses that do not require factories, physical products, shipping or shops. For example, the founders of the online photo-sharing site Instagram created a business with just thirteen employees, then sold it in 2012 for one billion dollars.

Is it any wonder people are interested in different business models?

In this chapter, you will

- learn vocabulary related to new business models;
- listen for the main idea;

- organize ideas using note-taking strategies;
- manage conversations and ask questions;
- review yes/no questions and information questions;

- participate in group discussions;
- give a presentation and take notes.

GEARING UP

A. Look at the diagram and then answer the questions.

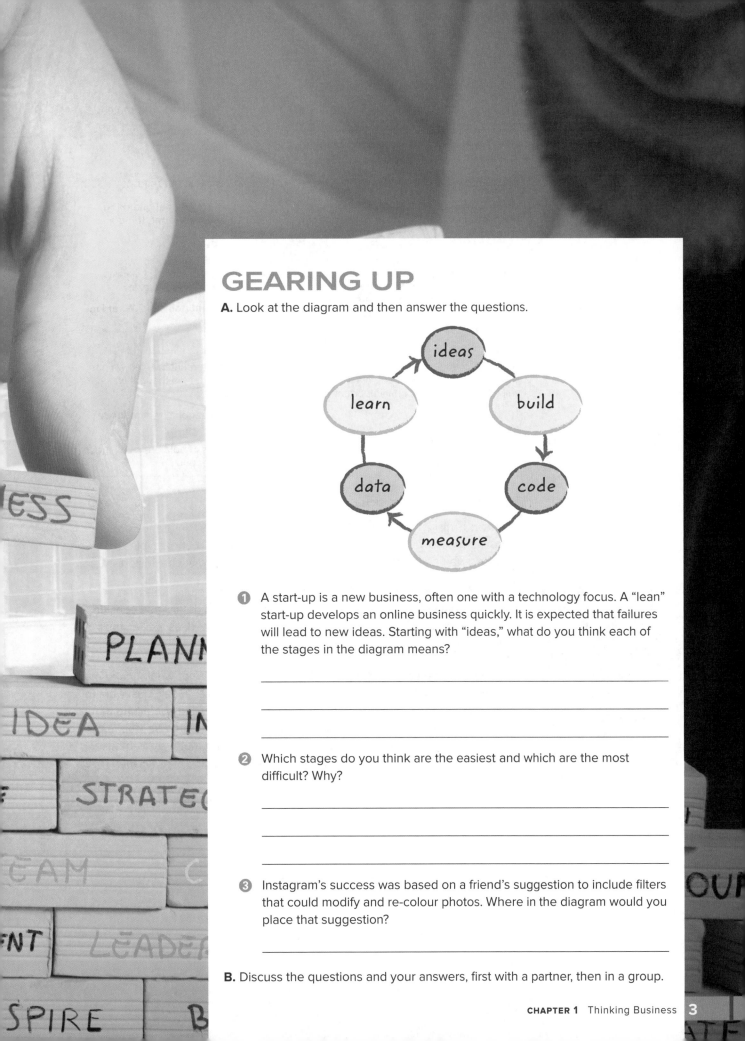

1. A start-up is a new business, often one with a technology focus. A "lean" start-up develops an online business quickly. It is expected that failures will lead to new ideas. Starting with "ideas," what do you think each of the stages in the diagram means?

   _____

   _____

   _____

2. Which stages do you think are the easiest and which are the most difficult? Why?

   _____

   _____

   _____

3. Instagram's success was based on a friend's suggestion to include filters that could modify and re-colour photos. Where in the diagram would you place that suggestion?

   _____

B. Discuss the questions and your answers, first with a partner, then in a group.

FOCUS ON LISTENING

Listening for the Main Idea

While you listen to a talk, try to identify the main idea. Sometimes the main idea is obvious; often, it is introduced in the title. Here are strategies you can use to help you identify a main idea while you listen.

STRATEGIES	EXPLANATIONS	EXAMPLES FROM LISTENING 1
Listen for words and ideas that are repeated.	A speaker says some words more frequently, or uses synonyms and paraphrases.	... we weren't great at one **thing**. Right, there wasn't one **thing** that was special ...
Listen for clues from the speaker that tell you some parts of a talk are more important.	A speaker asks questions that will be answered in the talk. A speaker uses words and phrases to indicate that one or more ideas are important.	And **the best** moment of all was, when things started to grow. **The important point is** ... **What I'm trying to say** ...
Listen for changes in pitch and volume.	Words spoken at a higher pitch or in a louder voice signal important ideas.	And we waited until we felt we had something that we thought was really **cool**. So, we're just going to **market** this thing. (Note: words in bold are said louder or at a higher pitch.)

These key phrases often signal main ideas.

INTRODUCTION: Today, we'll discuss ...   REPETITION: In other words, ...
EXCEPTION: However, ...   EXAMPLE: For example, ...
CAUSE AND EFFECT: Because of this, ...   SUMMARY: In conclusion, ...

A. Finding the main idea involves ignoring unnecessary details. Read this excerpt from Listening 1. Cross out words, phrases and details you consider unnecessary. Highlight important words that are repeated, as well as their synonyms.

> Somebody asked me once, like what's my big plan? What would make me really happy? When we were starting Pinterest I was like, "Geez, I just want to go somewhere and see somebody that I don't know using something that I made and have it be kind of useful." Like that is what I thought was really exciting. And so, we came up with this idea for something that was Web-based, really simple, something that we would use personally, and that was Pinterest.

B. Ignoring details and considering repeated words, what is the main idea of the paragraph in task A?

_____

_____

_____

_____

© **ERPI** • Reproduction prohibited

A. Below are words and phrases from the Academic Word List that you will find in Listening 1. Highlight the words you understand and then circle the words you use.

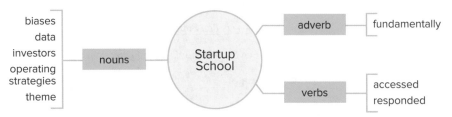

biases
data
investors
operating
strategies
theme

nouns → Startup School

adverb → fundamentally

verbs → accessed / responded

B. Match each word to its definition.

WORDS		DEFINITIONS
❶ accessed	_____	a) principles for running a company
❷ biases	_____	b) subject or idea behind something
❸ operating strategies	_____	c) obtained information
❹ theme	_____	d) prejudices against something

C. Fill in the blanks with the correct words to complete the paragraph. Use a dictionary to look up words you don't understand.

data	fundamentally	investors	responded

Throughout history, _____ have always _____ to market needs by supporting or developing new companies. They are _____ interested in creating profits for themselves and others. One way investors have been able to create profits is to take advantage of vast amounts of _____.

Ben Silbermann at Startup School

Those who follow technology news are fascinated with what are called *origin stories*. An origin story explains the steps involved in the creation of a new product that went on to be worth millions or billions of dollars. Pinterest, a company that Ben Silbermann co-founded, was valued at five billion in 2014—just four years after the Pinterest app became available. When you hear Pinterest's origin story in Listening 1, consider the steps that led to its success.

Before You Listen

A. Based on the excerpt you read in Focus on Listening (page 4), and on the title and introduction to Listening 1, which questions about Ben Silbermann would you expect to have answered? Write the questions and discuss them with a partner. Then, while you listen, take notes and use them to write complete answers.

1 Who *is Ben Silbermann?* _____

Ben Silbermann is a young entrepreneur who co-founded Pinterest. _____

2 What _____

_____

_____

3 When _____

_____

_____

4 Where _____

_____

_____

5 Why _____

_____

_____

6 How _____

_____

_____

B. What do you already know about technology start-ups? Discuss in a group.

_____

_____

C. Define the words and phrases in bold based on their context in the paragraph. Look at the surrounding words, definitions and examples. These words will help you understand Listening 1.

Many young entrepreneurs are attracted to California's **Silicon Valley** to work in the technology industry. Getting a job can be as easy as connecting with employers attending one or more **meetups**. At meetups, they can get together with technically minded people who have the necessary **engineering resources** to do an app's programming. Those who create apps tend to continue **iterating** an idea until they think it is ready for the market. It doesn't have to be the final version, but it has to reach the stage of being a **minimum viable product**. Only then are they ready to **launch**. Once they do, it's time to get people **jazzed** about it. This excitement can be generated through a **campaign**. In some cases, it helps to get a **blogger** to spread the news.

① Silicon Valley (n.): _____

_____

② meetups (n.): _____

_____

③ engineering resources (n.): _____

_____

④ iterating (v.): _____

_____

⑤ minimum viable product (n.): _____

_____

⑥ launch (v.): _____

_____

⑦ jazzed (adj.): _____

_____

⑧ campaign (n.): _____

_____

⑨ blogger (n.): _____

_____

While You Listen

D. Listen to a talk by young entrepreneur Ben Silbermann. The first time you listen, try to understand the main idea. Listen for words that are repeated, words that point out parts that are more important and changes in pitch and loudness. The talk consists of eight sections. The first sentence or phrase of each section is numbered below. While you listen the second time, choose the best main idea for each section. Listen a third time to check the main ideas and make corrections.

① Somebody asked me once, like what's my big plan?

    a) His plan is to work for a large and successful software company.

    b) Pinterest is the speaker's goal of a useful product that others want to use.

    c) He would like to make something exciting and useful, like Pinterest.

② We'd learned the lesson from doing the iPhone app …

    a) There is no point in launching a product you are not proud of.

    b) It's better to launch a product early and get feedback to improve.

    c) It's difficult to launch a product on your own; work together.

③ And we decided that the one thing we had to do really well …

    a) To succeed, the app needed to appeal to everyone.

    b) To succeed, the app had to be inexpensive.

    c) To succeed, the app had to be attractive.

④ So, this is the first version of Pinterest …

    a) Creating the final app depended on countless small improvements.

    b) The initial app turned out to be much the same as the final product.

    c) The trial version of the app was thrown out and they started over.

⑤ I e-mailed out all my friends, like all my family …

    a) It's better to change the product than find more users.

    b) It's better to find more users than change the product.

    c) Changing the product can help find more users.

⑥ And that's what we started to do …

    a) By not having any strategy, we were able to let people choose.

    b) It was important to see which strategies were successful elsewhere.

    c) Finding a strategy appropriate to the app was important.

⑦ So it was a really, really exciting moment for us.

    a) The app avoided dividing people according to their interests.

    b) The best part of the app was connecting people with their shared interests.

    c) The unexpected part was that most people didn't want to meet others.

⑧ A lot of people in Silicon Valley didn't get it.

    a) The app included a virtual booklet to explain the app's special features.

    b) Others expected the app to have the same features as other apps.

    c) Once an app is launched, everyone expects it to do as well as other apps.

After You Listen

E. Indicate whether these statements are true or false, according to the listening.

STATEMENTS	TRUE	FALSE
❶ Silbermann created Pinterest on his own.	☐	☑
❷ He wanted to create something that he would want to use.	☐	☐
❸ A new app has to have good features for you to get any feedback.	☐	☐
❹ Silbermann didn't show the app to anyone until it was launched.	☐	☐
❺ He tried to get his friends and family involved.	☐	☐
❻ Meetups were used to create a community of engineers.	☐	☐
❼ The word *genuine* is used to describe the connections that were made.	☐	☐
❽ It's important to listen to everyone else when designing a new app.	☐	☐

F. Now that you have identified the main idea for each section, what would you say is the main idea of the entire talk? Discuss this with a partner and then write the main idea below.

_____

_____

Academic
Survival Skill

Taking Notes

You take notes to help you remember the details of an assignment or lecture, or to have a record of a meeting so that you can bring up points and ask questions later. When your teacher offers additional explanations about something in your textbook, you can add notes to the particular section.

Taking notes helps to develop your listening skills. Learn to listen for main ideas and important details while blocking out information that doesn't matter. There are a number of ways to take notes including using mind maps, timelines or outlines.

Mind maps

Mind maps show relationships among ideas. Start with a central idea, such as the title of the lecture, and branch off to related ideas. In turn, the related ideas branch off further. If a topic changes, start a new mind map. One way to use a mind map is to write the topic in the centre circle with *who, what, when, where, why* and *how* circles branching off from it.

A. Look at this example of a mind map based on Listening 2. Based on the mind map, discuss with a partner what you think Listening 2 is about.

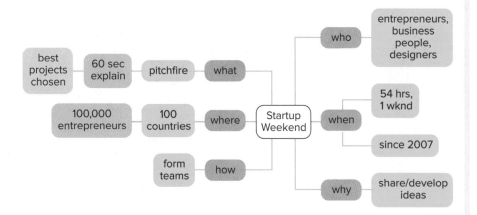

B. When you take notes, you don't have time to write everything the speaker says. Instead, write key words and use abbreviations and symbols: *sec, hrs* and *wknd* for *seconds, hours* and *weekend*. Write symbols you could use for the following terms.

MEANING	SYMBOL
greater than	>
less than	
equals/equal to	
not equal to	
connected ideas	
up/popular	
down/unpopular	

MEANING	SYMBOL
number	
dollars/money	
percent	
and/plus	
at	
essential information	
not clear/question	

© **ERPI** • Reproduction prohibited

Timelines

When a talk features several dates or refers to changes over time, take notes using a timeline. Draw a horizontal or vertical line on a page and add dates. While you listen, write short notes next to each date or point in time.

C. Fill in the timeline with these short notes from Listening 1.

- meetups
- desire to design app
- developed it with friends
- S. wanted an app he could use
- Pinterest success
- showed friends, family

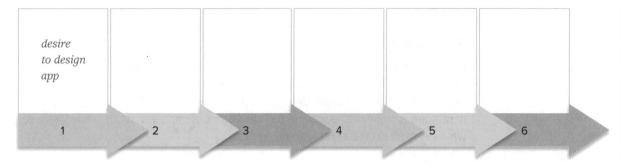

desire to design app

1   2   3   4   5   6

Outlines

Outlines work on the principle that main ideas are followed by supporting details. Look at this example. You will use this model to take notes in Listening 3.

Startup Weekend	• 2007
	– non-profit
	• Isaac Newton
	– work better in groups
	• entrepreneurs, business people, designers
	– meet 1 wknd/54 hrs
	– teams, develop prototype

VOCABULARY BUILD 2

A. Below are words from the Academic Word List that you will find in Listening 2. Highlight the words you understand and then circle the words you use.

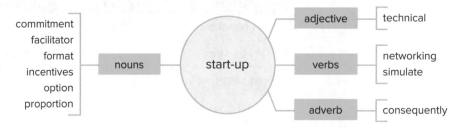

nouns: commitment, facilitator, format, incentives, option, proportion

start-up

adjective — technical

verbs — networking, simulate

adverb — consequently

B. Highlight the word in parentheses that best completes each sentence. Key words are in bold.

1 I don't want to make a **commitment** so I'll (choose / avoid) a date.

2 The new **facilitator** came to (organize / observe) the meeting.

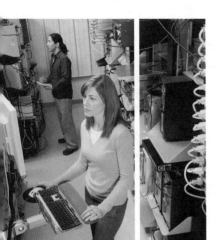

③ The company has a special e-mail **format** that (everyone / no one) must use.

④ The company provided many **incentives** to (inform / reward) employees.

⑤ She wanted to do everything in **proportion** and (balance / unbalance) things.

C. Synonyms are words that have similar meanings. Highlight the word or phrase that has the closest meaning to each word in bold.

① One last **option** is to get money from a venture capitalist.

    a) decision   b) dead end   c) possibility

② Wages were cut in half and **consequently** many people left the company.

    a) therefore   b) beforehand   c) unfortunately

③ Their idea of **networking** involved meeting people in the computer industry.

    a) wiring   b) connecting   c) spreading

④ The engineering plans were too **technical** for me to understand.

    a) unusual   b) important   c) scientific

⑤ The software program tries to **simulate** the feeling of meeting friends in person.

    a) recover   b) imitate   c) introduce

D. VOCABULARY EXTENSION: Some words have both noun and verb forms. Write definitions for these words.

WORDS	NOUN DEFINITIONS	VERB DEFINITIONS
① format	*way in which something is arranged*	
② network		
③ option		
④ proportion		

Fifty-four Hours: Startup Weekend

Imagine you have a great idea for a new business but don't know anyone with the technical skills to help you make it happen. What would you do? Startup Weekend has been answering that question since 2007 with weekend get-togethers in more than one hundred countries. Participants share ideas and form teams to work on bringing the more interesting ideas closer to reality—all in just a fifty-four hour period. In Listening 2, you will hear how some ideas might attract funding to get them started as real businesses.

music skills

baking skills

magic tricks

good with kids

HOST KIDS' BIRTHDAY PARTIES

Before You Listen

A. Form groups of six or more students. Ask each group member to write three or more skills he or she has, each one on a separate slip of paper. One member of the group collects and mixes these slips, then lays them out for everyone to see. In your group, look over the skills and make connections. Discuss how several skills could work together in a new business.

B. Fill in the blanks with the words that have the closest meaning to the words and phrases in bold. These words will help you understand Listening 2.

circulate	incessantly	iterations	pitch	prototype	skits

In funding meetings, **short performances** (_____) are often

used as icebreakers to get people to **move around** (_____)

and meet other people. If everyone moves **without stopping**

(_____), however, then there won't be any time to make

a **proposal** (_____). So there are **variations**

(_____) of icebreakers, such as ones where you stand

at a table with a **model** (_____) and people come to you.

While You Listen

C. While you listen to the interview, try to focus on both the questions and the answers. On the next page are Jeff Smith's interview questions. Take notes on Louise Fox's answers. Then, when the listening is finished, go back and add examples and explanations. Remember to use abbreviations when you take notes. You will hear the interview more than once, but take notes during the first listening, just as you might during a lecture.

SMITH'S QUESTIONS/COMMENTS	FOX'S ANSWERS/COMMENTS
Welcome, and today we're talking to Louise Fox who is working with Startup Weekend, an organization that's been around since 2004.	around since 2007
… It's sort of a meeting of geniuses and inventors, isn't it?	many innovations from groups Isaac Newton agreed
Did you say *giants*? What did he mean by giants?	
Got it! So tell us about Startup Weekend. Is it something that's going to change the world?	
Excuse me, just fifty-four? I heard that no one sleeps at these things!	
And I've heard it's been a success. Would you agree?	
Technical, design, business. Uh-huh.	Startup Weekend Friday night networking
I've heard it's expensive to attend, but you said it was a non-profit. Can you tell me where all the money goes?	question not answered
I understand that the teams are not just working on their own. Can you give me an example of the help they get?	coaches are Startup Weekend veterans
Let me cut in here. It seems they're very motivated. What do you think?	
Would you be able to tell me what the presentations consist of?	presentations consist of
Very impressive. For you, what would you say is the measure of success for Startup Weekend?	

After You Listen

D. Write short answers to these questions.

1 When did Startup Weekend first begin?

_____

2 Why is the scientist Isaac Newton mentioned?

_____

3 How many hours does Startup Weekend last?

_____

4 What is the measure of the success for Startup Weekend?

_____

5 What is the purpose of the Startup Weekend icebreaker activity?

_____

6 Why do you think Pitchfire's time limit is only sixty seconds?

_____

7 What is the purpose of the talks by experts?

_____

8 What is the reason for the many formats used in the final presentations?

_____

Isaac Newton (1643-1727) said he saw further by "standing on the shoulders of giants"—the scientists who came before him.

E. What would you expect to do at a Startup Weekend event? Number the following in order.

_____ ask for help from coaches

_____ form teams

_____ listen for winners of top prototypes and then celebrate and network

_____ listen to a short speech by the facilitator

___1___ network over dinner

_____ vote on best and most viable ideas

_____ prepare for a late-afternoon presentation and then respond to questions

_____ participate in an icebreaker

_____ share ideas in a Pitchfire session

_____ work together in teams, taking breaks to eat and drink

F. Based on your notes and answers to task D, what is the main idea of Startup Weekend? Discuss in a group.

FOCUS ON SPEAKING

Managing a Conversation

Sometimes you are asked to listen without interrupting, such as in a lecture. Other times you are involved in the discussion and are expected to participate. An important part of participating is managing the conversation. These strategies can help improve your understanding of what is being said and allow you to contribute more effectively.

A. Read the strategies and practise the example conversation with a partner. Write phrases of your own in the empty squares in task B.

STRATEGIES	PURPOSE	EXAMPLE CONVERSATION
ASK FOR A RESPONSE	Make sure everyone is engaged in the conversation.	Do you agree? What's your opinion? What do you think?
ASK FOR MORE DETAIL	Find out more information.	Could you explain that? How exactly does that work?
ASK FOR CLARIFICATION	Find out the meaning of a word or other detail.	So you're saying that ... Let me get this straight ... I'm not sure what you mean by ... Are you sure?
EXPRESS AN OPINION	Share an idea even though it may not be supported by facts.	I don't agree. That seems wrong. That doesn't seem right to me.
POLITELY INTERRUPT	Make space in the conversation for your questions or point of view.	Excuse me, but my point is ... Before you go on, could I add ... Please, let me say something here.

My eLab
Visit My eLab Documents for additional strategies for managing a conversation.

B. In a small group, discuss which of your courses will most likely help you get a job. During the conversation, try to use each strategy at least once. Keep your book open to this page and when one of your group members uses one of the strategies, be the first to point to it.

ask for a response		ask for more detail	
ask for clarification	express an opinion		politely interrupt

Pronunciation: To improve your pronunciation, record what you hear; then, record yourself repeating it and compare the two.

C. With your group, discuss which strategies were used more often and which strategies were seldom used, and why.

Yes/No Questions

You have already seen questions that ask *who, what, when, where, why* and *how*. These types of questions are called information questions. Information questions ask for information by using question words that encourage short specific answers. But when you want the briefest answer possible, ask questions that have *yes* or *no* answers.

VERB *to be*	SUBJECT	PHRASE	ANSWERS
Are Aren't	you	networking?	Yes, I am (networking). No, I'm not (networking).
Is Isn't	she	Louise Fox?	Yes, she is (Louise Fox). No, she's not (Louise Fox).
Am Aren't	I	late?	Yes, you are (late). No, you aren't (late).
VERB *to do*	**SUBJECT**	**PHRASE**	**ANSWERS**
Do Don't	you	know Louise?	Yes, I do (know Louise). No, I don't (know Louise).
Does Doesn't	he	network?	Yes, he does (network). No, he doesn't (network).
Did Didn't	they	finish?	Yes, they did (finish). No, they didn't (finish).
VERB *to have*	**SUBJECT**	**PHRASE**	**ANSWERS**
Has Hasn't	he	networked?	Yes, he has (networked). No, he hasn't (networked).
Have Haven't	you	met Louise?	Yes, I have (met Louise). No, I haven't (met Louise).
Has Hasn't	the group	finished?	Yes, the group has (finished). No, the group hasn't (finished).

> ❶ When people speak quickly, they often blend the final sound of one word together with the first sound of another. Listen carefully to understand the individual words.

A. Change these information questions to *yes* or *no* questions.

❶ Who offers the workshops?

_____

❷ What has made your company more efficient?

_____

❸ When did you start your company?

_____

❹ Where is your company located?

_____

❺ Why did you start a company?

_____

> ❶ Use what you learned about yes/no questions when you prepare assignments.

❻ How do people volunteer with you?

_____

B. Practise asking and answering the questions with a partner.

WARM-UP ASSIGNMENT
Create and Present an Idea for an Application

In this Warm-Up Assignment, you will work in groups to create an idea for a new application.

The following are among the most popular applications downloaded for mobile phones.

- banking
- communication
- entertainment
- food
- games

- maps
- music
- news
- productivity
- shopping

- social networking
- sports
- travel
- video
- weather

A. Form groups of three. From the list above, work together to combine two or more of the applications to create an idea for a new one. For example, you might combine *social networking + banking* to compete with friends on ways to save money, or you might combine *weather + maps + entertainment* to play a game to learn about different kinds of clouds.

B. Discuss your ideas. Use the conversation strategies you learned in Focus on Speaking (page 15). Ask questions about different applications and how they work (refer to Focus on Grammar).

C. Present your application to the class and briefly explain it. Each group member should talk about one part of the process. For example, one member might explain how the idea came about. A second member might introduce the application itself, demonstrating how it will work. A third member might give evidence of how the application could solve a problem, or how it could be used to learn something new.

D. After your presentation, ask for feedback from your teacher and classmates. Use this feedback to improve your application or your presentation. You will revise your presentation for the Final Assignment.

**VOCABULARY
BUILD 3**

A. Below are words from the Academic Word List that you will find in Listening 3. Highlight the words you understand and then circle the words you use.

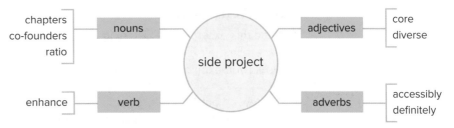

chapters
co-founders
ratio — **nouns**

enhance — **verb**

side project

adjectives — core
diverse

adverbs — accessibly
definitely

B. Choose the phrase that best completes each sentence. Key words are in bold.

① She established **chapters** in each city so members could _____.

   a) read parts of books

   b) get together

   c) work alone

2 The **core** members of the workshops _____.

   a) were not good programmers

   b) attended one session

   c) were the instructors

3 An **accessibly** priced package meant _____.

   a) no one could afford it

   b) everyone could afford it

   c) everyone could find out the cost

4 As **co-founders** of the company they _____.

   a) were also in charge of it

   b) had to answer to others

   c) could only volunteer

C. Highlight the word that has the closest meaning to each word in bold.

1 The **ratio** of instructors to students is one to four.

   a) total   b) proportion   c) remainder

2 The organization had several **diverse** plans to teach software.

   a) different   b) similar   c) traditional

3 To **enhance** service, the organization looked for passionate employees.

   a) reduce   b) ignore   c) improve

4 Programming workshops were **definitely** needed for those with no coding experience.

   a) temporarily   b) certainly   c) possibly

Visit My eLab to complete Vocabulary Review exercises for this chapter.

Hack to Start: Heather Payne

Young entrepreneur Heather Payne founded Ladies Learning Code, a not-for-profit start-up that runs inexpensive workshops teaching computer programming and other technical skills. The start-up was a side project—an idea outside her normal work. Many people have ideas for side projects but do not act on them. Payne suggests that this is because they lose momentum, or the desire to move forward.

Before You Listen

A. Read this excerpt from Listening 3. In it Payne talks about how she got started. Based on the excerpt, and on the title and the introduction, which questions would you expect to have answered? Write the questions and the answers.

> I grew up outside of Toronto, in Brampton, and went to Western to study business, so I graduated with a business degree in 2009, and that whole time actually, entrepreneurship wasn't really something that I was necessarily interested in. I went through all of university thinking that I would join, you know, like a company, and work my way up or something like that. And it wasn't until after I graduated, and I guess, you know, really realized that I preferred smaller companies, because you get to be more of a generalist.

1 Who *is the speaker?* _____

The speaker is Heather Payne. _____

2 What _____

_____

3 When _____

_____

4 Where _____

_____

5 Why _____

_____

6 How _____

_____

B. In the speech, Payne talks about setting up coding workshops for women. Why might she have been more interested in having the workshops for women rather than for men or for a mixed group?

_____

_____

C. These words and phrases will help you understand Listening 3. Read each statement and use the context to match the word or phrase in bold to its meaning. Discuss your answers with a partner.

STATEMENTS		MEANINGS
1 As a **generalist**, she was in demand everywhere.	_____	a) dissatisfied
2 He tried to walk straight to the front, but **stumbled**.	_____	b) gossip or casual talk
3 I'm **passionate** about coding; it's my whole life.	_____	c) lost footing or balance
4 I was unable to do it at first and became **frustrated**.	_____	d) natural development
5 The first coding she did was with **Python**.	_____	e) initiated
6 It wasn't planned; the project had an **organic growth**.	_____	f) one who can do everything
7 As the team leader, she **spearheaded** the new project.	_____	g) coding language
8 We heard by **word of mouth**, not from what we read.	_____	h) deeply interested

Develop Your Vocabulary: When speakers use words or phrases you don't know, politely interrupt to clarify: "Do you mean ...?"

While You Listen

D. The first time you listen, try to get the main idea. Listen a second time for key words. Use the outline technique from Academic Survival Skill (page 9) to take notes. Listen a third time to check your notes and add details.

NARRATOR: Can you tell us a little bit about yourself?

• grew up Brampton

• _____

_____

– _____

_____

– _____

_____

– _____

_____

– _____

_____

NARRATOR: How did you decide to start this organization?

• 2009 the economy had collapsed

• _____

_____

– _____

_____

– _____

_____

LOS ANGELES: For work; joined workshop for women to learn Python.

• idea to have workshops in Toronto

• _____

_____

– _____

_____

– _____

_____

– _____

NARRATOR: How did you actually hack the growth for Ladies Learning Code?

• 19 chapters in less than three years

• _____
_____
• _____
_____
– _____
_____
– _____
_____
– Melissa Cernic _____
_____
– _____
_____

TWITTER: Participants helped promote the workshops.

• _____
_____
– _____
_____
– _____
_____

OTHER CITIES: Not difficult.

• _____
_____

After You Listen

E. Highlight the word or phrase in parentheses that best completes each sentence.

1. Heather Payne graduated from Western University in (programming / business).

2. After graduating, she decided to (get a job / travel).

3. A group in Los Angeles (inspired / borrowed) the idea of Ladies Learning Code.

4. In Toronto, she co-founded Ladies Learning Code, an organization to teach (programming / business).

⑤ After starting in Toronto, the next city to host workshops was (Vancouver / Ottawa).

⑥ The low cost plus lunch are two reasons the workshops are (profitable / popular).

⑦ Each city's workshops are organized by (Payne / core members).

⑧ Payne (no longer / still) heads Ladies Learning Code.

F. Choose the best summary of Listening 3.

☐ Heather Payne was inspired by the Los Angeles group Ladies Learning Code to teach herself coding and start a business teaching others how to build and program computers.

☐ Heather Payne's interest in business made her look for an opportunity in which she could compete against other groups delivering programming training to Canadian women.

☐ After Heather Payne learned to code, she decided it was a skill that could benefit other women so she set up enjoyable workshops that now continue without her involvement.

FINAL ASSIGNMENT
Give a Presentation and Take Notes

Use what you learned in this chapter to deliver a revised version of the presentation you first gave in the Warm-Up Assignment. You will also take notes on the presentations of other groups.

A. Re-form your Warm-Up Assignment groups.

B. Based on the feedback you received from your teacher and classmates, consider how you can improve your Warm-Up Assignment application or presentation and make revisions.

C. Follow the same procedure and divide the revised presentation among group members. When you have finished, ask for feedback.

D. While you listen to your classmates' presentations, take notes using symbols and a mind map, a timeline or an outline format (see Academic Survival Skill, page 9).

E. While you listen, write your feedback questions, comments and suggestions. Depending on the response you need, ask either yes/no questions or information questions with *who*, *what*, *when*, *where*, *why* and *how* question words (see Focus on Grammar, page 16). If you need to interrupt a presentation, do so politely.

F. When presentations are finished, as a class, vote for the best application. A group cannot vote for its own application.

How confident
are you?

Think about what you learned in this chapter. Use the table to decide what you should review.

I LEARNED ...	I AM CONFIDENT	I NEED TO REVIEW
vocabulary related to new business models;	☐	☐
to listen for the main idea;	☐	☐
how to organize ideas using note-taking strategies;	☐	☐
how to manage conversations and ask questions;	☐	☐
about yes/no questions and information questions;	☐	☐
how to participate in group discussions;	☐	☐
how to give a presentation.	☐	☐

VOCABULARY
Challenge

Think about the vocabulary and ideas in this chapter. Use these words to write two sentences about new business models.

commitment	conducive	incentives	initiatives	innovative	visionary

_____

_____

_____

_____

_____

My eLab

Visit My eLab to build on what you learned.

CHAPTER 2

A New World of Work

The question, "What do you want to do when you grow up?," is one you probably heard as a child, but as you grow older, it's increasingly difficult to answer. In past centuries, children were often trained for the occupations of their parents, who, similarly, were taught by their parents. Education has since broadened the job options for many young people, but it can be difficult both to choose subjects to study and to choose a career after.

If you could have your perfect job, what would it be?

In this chapter, you will

- learn vocabulary related to jobs;
- use active listening strategies;
- review comparative and superlative adjectives;

- use intonation and stress;
- give a descriptive presentation;
- learn compare and contrast presentation structure;

- learn about citations and references in presentations;
- give a compare and contrast presentation with a partner.

GEARING UP

A. Look at the diagram and then answer the questions.

Predicted shortages and surpluses for university graduates in the workplace

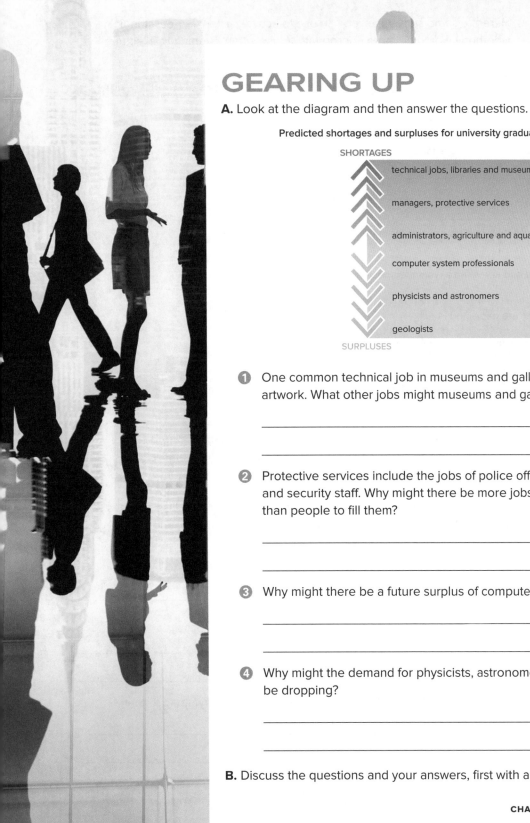

SHORTAGES

technical jobs, libraries and museums

managers, protective services

administrators, agriculture and aquaculture

computer system professionals

physicists and astronomers

geologists

SURPLUSES

❶ One common technical job in museums and galleries is restoring artwork. What other jobs might museums and galleries need filled?

_____

_____

❷ Protective services include the jobs of police officers, firefighters and security staff. Why might there be more jobs in these areas than people to fill them?

_____

_____

❸ Why might there be a future surplus of computer professionals?

_____

_____

❹ Why might the demand for physicists, astronomers and geologists be dropping?

_____

_____

B. Discuss the questions and your answers, first with a partner, then in a group.

FOCUS ON LISTENING

Using Active Listening Strategies

When you listen, whether it is to a formal lecture or a casual conversation, you need to listen actively. Active listening means focused listening: paying close attention to what is being said and showing that you are listening.

A. What purposes do you have when you listen to lectures and take part in conversations? Discuss with a partner.

B. Here are some strategies you can use to actively listen. For each, indicate whether it would be more appropriate to use when listening to a lecture or to a conversation, or both.

LISTENING STRATEGIES	LECTURE	CONVERSATION	BOTH
1 Make eye contact and use non-verbal body language to show you're interested in what the speaker has to say.			
2 Listen patiently, but interrupt to ask questions when you do not understand.			
3 Listen for ways in which the speaker's ideas fit or conflict with your own.			
4 Avoid distractions; ensure that your phone and other devices are off.			
5 Take notes, paraphrase and summarize what the speaker says.			
6 Give the speaker the benefit of the doubt, not rejecting anything that is said until all ideas are explained in full.			
7 Interact with the speaker with sounds or body language that show you agree or disagree, or that you are confused.			
8 After, reflect on what you have heard and modify your ideas or notes, adding your own interpretations of what has been said.			

Active listening often involves asking questions to clarify. Sometimes you ask closed-ended questions to get a *yes* or *no* answer. Other times, you ask open-ended questions that encourage the speaker to share more.

C. Rewrite these questions to make them more open-ended. Use phrases such as, "What do you mean ...," "What makes you think ..." and "Could you explain ..."

1 Have you reached a conclusion?

Could you explain your conclusion?

2 By new jobs, do you mean technology jobs?

_____

_____

3 Nobody believes there will be 50 percent unemployment, do they?

_____

_____

④ Everyone knows cashier jobs are on the way out, right?

_____

_____

⑤ So are you saying that it would be foolish to work in heavy industry?

_____

_____

VOCABULARY
BUILD 1

A. Below are words from the Academic Word List that you will find in Listening 1. Highlight the words you understand and then circle the words you use.

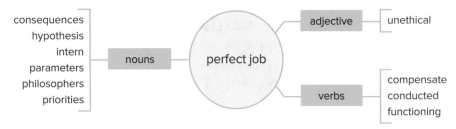

consequences
hypothesis
intern
parameters
philosophers
priorities

nouns

perfect job

adjective — unethical

verbs — compensate
conducted
functioning

B. Choose the word or phrase in parentheses that best completes each sentence. Key words are in bold.

① The company chose an **intern** as a (temporary / permanent) summer helper.

② Her **hypothesis** on the future of jobs was an educated (fact / guess).

③ To avoid any **consequences**, she did (nothing / something).

④ The **philosophers** gathered to discuss several debatable (ideas / facts).

⑤ One of the **parameters** was a tight deadline, so they had (lots of time / thirty minutes).

C. Fill in the blanks with the correct words to complete the sentences.

compensate	conducted	functioning	priorities	unethical

① It's both illegal and _____ to pay people less than minimum wage.

② Many experiments were _____ to determine students' work preferences.

③ Although many of her old websites don't work, some are still

_____.

④ In setting _____, many companies decide that making money comes first.

⑤ Good companies _____ employees fairly with a mix of pay and benefits.

The Perfect Job

Many people feel fortunate to have a job and do not consider leaving it to start another, especially if that next job has a higher degree of risk. Working for yourself has many benefits to do with independence, but it also means you may not have the safety net that working for a large company provides. Yet more and more people make the decision to work for themselves, hoping that the benefits will outweigh the costs. Listening 1 sets out some ideas to help you consider what would make your perfect job.

Before You Listen

A. Think of three jobs you might like to have in future. Discuss your choices in a group, defining the qualities of a perfect job. Then, vote to decide on the three best jobs.

B. Read the following excerpt from Listening 1. How and why might your idea of a perfect job change over time?

> Let's agree that there's no such thing as a single perfect job that suits everyone. For example, many people might like to lead an important company, but would ultimately object to the stress of great responsibility. We should also recognize that people's ideas of a perfect job change over time.

_____

_____

_____

C. These words will help you understand Listening 1. Match each to its definition.

WORDS		DEFINITIONS
❶ mental gymnastics	_____	a) finally
❷ vegan	_____	b) lacking skill or prestige
❸ ultimately	_____	c) everlasting
❹ autonomy	_____	d) problem-solving exercises
❺ perpetual	_____	e) independence
❻ menial	_____	f) neither eating nor using animal products

Develop Your Vocabulary: Words like "improbable" (unlikely) and "implausible" (unconvincing) are similar but have different meanings. To improve your vocabulary, identify differences between synonyms.

While You Listen

D. Read the items in the first column to understand some of the parameters, or boundaries, of the perfect job. Then, listen and take notes on each one. Listen a second time to check your answers and then a third time to reflect on your notes, modifying them by adding your own interpretations.

PARAMETERS	NOTES
no such thing as a single perfect job	*No one job would suit everyone.*
change itself	
independence and intellectual stimulation	
high degree of autonomy	
emotional rewards	
exceptional skills	
money	
supply and demand	
education of skilled workers	
altruism	

After You Listen

E. Indicate whether these statements are true or false, according to the listening.

STATEMENTS	TRUE	FALSE
1 The thought experiment is a problem-solving technique that predates the scientific method.	☐	☐
2 Thought experiments are not conducted in the physical world.	☐	☐
3 Thought experiments were never used to explore what might have been solved by a simple experiment.	☐	☐
4 Thought experiments are conducted because an actual experiment is not practical.	☐	☐
5 Unethical hypotheses are never debated as thought experiments.	☐	☐
6 Thought experiments are sometimes used to examine the impossible.	☐	☐
7 The lecture's thought experiment is used to investigate a work-related hypothesis.	☐	☐
8 The hypothesis of the lecture's thought experiment was accepted.	☐	☐
9 Even a rejected thought experiment can be successful if it leads to new ideas.	☐	☐

F. Explain the importance of each of these examples. Why does the lecturer mention each one? Discuss your answers with a partner.

① having students intern at a hundred different jobs to gauge the influence on their choice of careers: _____

_____

② forcing a group of people to take on jobs that they hate, simply to observe their performance: _____

_____

③ imagining people's lives and jobs in a vegan society where animals were freed from having to work or produce food for humans: _____

_____

④ leading an important company: _____

_____

⑤ being a surfing instructor: _____

_____

⑥ creating magazine travel articles: _____

_____

⑦ being a symphony conductor or an astronaut: _____

_____

⑧ cleaning sewers: _____

_____

FOCUS ON GRAMMAR

Comparative and Superlative Form

In Listening 1, you heard phrases like "my older self" and "the most dangerous jobs." Adjectives (e.g., *old, dangerous*) describe nouns and adverbs describe verbs. Comparatives (e.g., *older, more dangerous*) compare two nouns or verbs, saying which is more or less than the other. Superlatives (e.g., *oldest, most dangerous*) describe nouns or verbs as being the most or least of three or more things.

A. Read the rules for how to form comparative and superlative adjectives. Then, write a second example.

RULES	COMPARATIVE	SUPERLATIVE
for one-syllable adjectives, ending in -e EXAMPLE: safe	add *-r + than* safe**r than** _____	put *the* before the adjective and add *-st* **the** safe**st** _____
for one-syllable adjectives, ending in a consonant EXAMPLE: hot	double the consonant and add *-er + than* hot**ter than** _____	put *the* before the adjective, double the consonant and add *-est* **the** hot**test** _____

RULES	COMPARATIVE	SUPERLATIVE
for two-syllable adjectives, ending in -y EXAMPLE: happy	change the y to i and add -er + than happ**ier than** _____	put *the* before the adjective, change *y* to *i* and add -*est* **the** happ**iest** _____
for two or more syllables, not ending in -y EXAMPLE: realistic	put *more* before and *than* after the adjective **more** realistic **than** _____	put *the most* before the adjective **the most** realistic _____

B. Some irregular adjectives have different forms of comparatives and superlatives. They are exceptions to the rules. You need to memorize them. Fill in the missing words.

ADJECTIVES	COMPARATIVE	SUPERLATIVE
_____	worse	worst
good	_____	best
_____	less	least
much	_____	most
far	farther (distance) / further (time)	_____ (distance) / (time)

C. Change the adjective in parentheses to either the comparative or the superlative form.

1 He had (good, superlative) _____ reason for finishing his degree.

2 We had (fine, superlative) _____ interns working for the new company.

3 Their new jobs were (interesting, comparative) _____

_____ their old ones.

4 She told me to put (little, comparative) _____ emphasis on looking for a job.

5 Technology start-ups tend to feature (trendy, superlative) _____

_____ jobs.

6 The boys were (busy, comparative) _____ the girls.

Use what you learned about comparatives and superlatives when you prepare assignments.

A. Below are words from the Academic Word List that you will find in Listening 2. Highlight the words you understand and then circle the words you use.

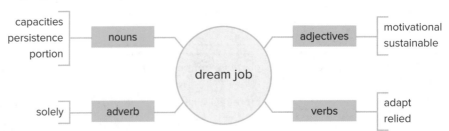

	nouns			adjectives	
capacities persistence portion					motivational sustainable

dream job

| solely | adverb | | | verbs | adapt relied |

B. Highlight the word or phrase that has the closest meaning to each word or phrase in bold.

❶ Her **persistence** in practising day after day paid off with a gold medal.

   a) savings   b) determination   c) relaxed attitude

❷ He took only a small **portion** of the food, knowing that others would want some.

   a) share   b) investment   c) total

❸ As a **motivational** speaker, his job was to get people working harder.

   a) loud and rude   b) judgmental   c) inspirational

❹ I have always **relied on** the kindness of strangers.

   a) regretted   b) trusted in   c) been cautious about

C. Fill in the blanks with the correct words to complete the paragraph.

adapt	capabilities	solely	sustainable

Universities cannot _____ focus on doing things the way they've always been done. A key concept in many universities is the idea of making things _____. This is done by looking at ways to ensure that the university can _____ to future challenges. They need to develop a variety of _____ to attract new students, retain old ones and prepare them all for life beyond university.

D. VOCABULARY EXTENSION: The suffix -*able* turns some verbs into adjectives. Change these verbs into adjectives by adding -*able*. If the verb ends in -*y*, change the *y* to *i*; if the verb ends in -*e*, drop the *e*.

VERBS		ADJECTIVES
❶	adapt	
❷	afford	
❸	compare	
❹	deplore	

VERBS		ADJECTIVES
❺	like	
❻	rely	
❼	sustain	
❾	vary	

Students Create Their Own Dream Jobs

A new approach to developing businesses is the *innovation incubator*. It is based on inviting individuals or groups to bring new business ideas to a group of experienced mentors (advisors) who can help develop the ideas. Often, part of this process includes competition: the individuals or groups with the best ideas get funding. This format has become common in the business world, as well as on TV. In Listening 2, you will hear how a version of this approach is being used at a college.

Before You Listen

A. One of the proposed businesses in Listening 2 is a motivational musician's plan to make money by charging for appearances at schools. If you were a mentor, what questions would you have about this kind of business? Write four questions and then discuss them with a partner.

1. _____

2. _____

3. _____

4. _____

B. Read this excerpt from Listening 2. In it, the narrator describes the motivation for students to become involved in the innovation incubator. Why might students prefer to create their dream jobs rather than wait for them?

> With media students producing it, Humber College's LaunchPad Competition is a live test of nerves: an innovation incubator where current students and recent grads compete for cash to finance their own businesses. Some have already tested out the job market, but no one here has found their dream job, or is willing to wait for it. They want to create it.

_____

_____

C. These words will help you understand Listening 2. Highlight the word or phrase in parentheses that best completes the sentence. Key words are in bold.

1. **Aquaculture**, farming fish and other sea life, is a (limited / sustainable practice).

2. They were **deluded** because they believed in things that (would / wouldn't) happen.

3. **Hydroponics** involves growing plants without (soil / water).

4. There was a **looming** deadline that meant they had (to finish quickly / lots of time).

5. A **nutrient-based** product was used to (take away / add to) the plants' food.

6. The company **preps** its employees so they (are ready / don't have) to make sales.

While You Listen

D. The first time you listen, try to understand the general idea. Before you listen a second time, read these questions. While you listen the second time, take notes on a separate page to help you answer the questions. Answer the questions, then listen a third time to check your answers and fill in details.

1 When the first woman says that the unemployment rate among recent graduates is "pretty dismal," what does she mean?

_____

_____

2 What is one problem with the job market?

_____

_____

3 Craig Petton and Pablos Havaras have jobs. Why are they anxious to change?

_____

_____

4 Why do Lindsay Branton and Brennan Lundy want to start their own business?

_____

_____

5 What is unusual about artist Colin Edwards' job idea?

_____

_____

6 What is the reason for competitions that ask students to do things like come up with a social media plan?

_____

_____

7 At the Humber innovation incubator, what is the role of the panel of judges?

_____

_____

8 How much were Lindsay and Brennan asking for and how much did they get?

_____

_____

9 Which group won the competition and how much did they get?

_____

_____

After You Listen

E. Write the details of the businesses associated with the following people.

1 Craig Petton and Pablos Havaras: _____

_____

2 Lindsay Branton and Brennan Lundy: _____

_____

3 Colin Edwards: _____

_____

4 Lauren Friese: _____

_____

F. Answer these questions. With a partner, discuss what each answer might mean to you.

1 Why does the narrator use the words *dreamers*, *risk-takers* and *optimists* to describe the students?

_____

_____

2 Why is this generation different?

_____

_____

_____

3 Why is entrepreneurship risky?

_____

_____

_____

4 What is the importance of learning to compete in business?

_____

_____

_____

5 Why does Friese mention the idea of standing out?

_____

_____

6 Why is persistence important?

_____

_____

> ❶
> *Pronunciation: As you gather your thoughts or think of how to pronounce a word, try to avoid filling the pause with "um" or "ah."*
> *It's better to look away for a moment.*

Using Intonation and Stress

When you speak, it's important to add intonation and stress to your words and sentences. *Intonation* refers to the rise and fall of your voice as you speak. For example, when you ask a question, your voice usually rises on the last word. *Stress* refers to the emphasis you put on different parts (syllables) of words. Sometimes stress on different syllables changes the meaning of a word, such as the noun *sub*ject and the verb sub*ject*.

A. Write a second sentence for each word. The stress falls on the first syllable for the noun form and on the second syllable for the verb form. Practise saying each sentence with a partner.

1 address (n.): The address is on Broadway.

address (v.): _____

_____

2 conduct (n.): The conduct of the team was excellent.

conduct (v.): _____

_____

3 conflict (n.): The war zone conflict is increasing.

conflict (v.): _____

_____

4 decrease (n.): We saw a decrease in waste.

decrease (v.): _____

_____

5 permit (n.): I have a permit to build the house.

permit (v.): _____

_____

6 record (n.): The record shows that she is innocent.

record (v.): _____

_____

B. Punctuation signals changes in intonation. Commas, semicolons and colons signal short pauses, and periods signal longer pauses. Practise saying these sentences with a partner.

• Every job, I think, has someone who would love to fill it.

• Here's an idea: everyone can have a perfect job.

• What would be different?

• So, the coolest thing is you can choose what you want, can't you?

• It's good to schedule ten or fifteen minutes, every day, as a time to think.

My eLab

You can listen to these sentences on My eLab Documents and compare your pronunciation.

WARM-UP ASSIGNMENT
Describe Your Perfect Job

Listenings 1 and 2 focused on defining the perfect job. In this Warm-Up Assignment, you will give a presentation describing your perfect job.

A. Begin by choosing your topic. Consider some of the factors that would make a job perfect for you: the kind of skills needed, the hours and duties required, the working conditions and the amount of pay expected. Ask your teacher to approve your choice.

B. Write an outline of your presentation. When you explain why your job is the best or what makes your perfect job better than other jobs, use comparative and superlative adjectives (see Focus on Grammar, page 30). For example,

> Being an astronaut is **better than** being a pilot because your trips can last for weeks, not hours. **The greatest** thing about being an astronaut is having a view of the world that few experience.

C. Practise your presentation on your own and with a partner. Then, present to the class. You can use key words to help you present, but do not read from your notes. Make eye contact and use body language to show your enthusiasm for your topic. When you speak, vary your intonation and stress (see Focus on Speaking).

D. While you listen to other students' presentations, use the active listening strategies you learned in Focus on Listening (page 26): ask questions and take notes so that you will be prepared to give feedback.

My eLab

Visit My eLab Documents for suggestions on effective presentations.

E. Once everyone has presented, ask for feedback from your teacher and classmates on how you could improve your presentation.

VOCABULARY BUILD 3

A. Below are words and phrases from the Academic Word List that you will find in Listening 3. Highlight the words you understand and then circle the words you use.

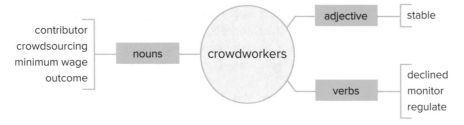

B. Choose the phrase that best completes each sentence. Key words are in bold.

❶ The **contributor** to the magazine _____.

   a) delivered copies to the store

   b) wrote articles for publication

   c) performed editorial duties

2 Many people want a **stable** job that _____.

    a) they may only do for a short time

    b) is a kind of seasonal employment

    c) stays the same year after year

3 The principle of a **minimum wage** is _____.

    a) to ensure that workers can afford to live

    b) so employers do not have to pay extra

    c) to avoid paying what is naturally fair

4 Businesses use **crowdsourcing** when they need _____.

    a) permanent staff to work on ideas

    b) to find one or two select employees

    c) many people helping with a project

C. Highlight the best definition for each word. Use a dictionary to check your answers.

1	regulate	a) give up on something	b) control or supervise something
2	monitor	a) observe a process or activity	b) plan to review activities
3	outcome	a) result	b) preparation
4	declined	a) accepted	b) refused

Visit My eLab to complete Vocabulary Review exercises for this chapter.

LISTENING ❸ Crowdworkers

In 1770, a chess-playing robot called the Mechanical Turk became a popular attraction in Europe. The robot, placed at a chess table, would play a game against skilful players and usually win. However, it was later shown to be a hoax: an expert human player hid inside the machine. The term *mechanical turk* or *m-turk* is now used for workers who work online completing small writing and programming tasks. In Listening 3, mechanical turks (turkers) are interviewed to find out about the advantages and disadvantages of their jobs.

Before You Listen

A. Google's chief executive officer Larry Page believes that the future of employment—for everyone—will be part-time. Many of us will have jobs that can be done online and will allow us to work from different locations for short periods of time. With a partner, discuss jobs that could fit this new model. Talk about other jobs that would not fit the model.

B. The opening paragraph of Listening 3 points out the issue of questionable labour practices. What problems might there be, in terms of pay and working conditions, for individuals working online doing mini-tasks?

> The Internet makes it easier for an individual to work at home, but it goes beyond that. Now, businesses can break down an individual's job into fragmented mini-tasks that can be done by many people scattered all over the world. And the explosion of this crowdsourced online micro-work has led to some questionable labour practices.

_____

_____

_____

C. It's sometimes difficult to know the meaning of a phrase from its individual words. These phrases are important for your understanding of Listening 3. Highlight the best definition for each. Use a dictionary to look up those that are unfamiliar.

1. grizzly details   a) unpleasant facts   b) bare necessities

2. decent living   a) proper behaviour   b) having enough to live on

3. enviable lifestyle   a) being always jealous   b) kind of life others want

4. legitimate way   a) workable solution   b) illegal move

5. class actions   a) group legal cases   b) strikes by students

6. green light   a) traffic warning   b) permission to proceed

7. industrial revolution   a) machine labour   b) robot attack

8. tide me over   a) overcome by waves   b) have enough to survive temporarily

While You Listen

D. The first time you listen, try to get the general idea. Listen a second time and take notes on each segment. Focus on the main message and consider whether the explanations and examples support the speakers' main ideas. Listen a third time to check your notes and add details.

SEGMENTS	NOTES
working flexible hours anywhere with a Wi-Fi connection	
Bateman avoids some crowdsourcing platforms.	
Mechanical Turk is	
Turker Nation works for	

SEGMENTS	NOTES
Researchers speculate turkers make as little as two dollars an hour.	
Ira Spiro is suing CrowdFlower, a competitor of Mechanical Turk.	
Hall of Fame or Shame	
A smart turker pays attention to self-worth and value of skills to make money.	*M-Turk offers options to make stable money.*

After You Listen

E. Review your notes and answer these questions. Then, discuss your answers with a partner.

1 What is an example of a kind of job a turker does?

_____

2 What are the benefits of working as a turker?

_____

3 What are the disadvantages of working as a turker?

_____

4 Why is Ira Spiro launching a class action suit against CrowdFlower?

_____

5 What is an ethical reason for avoiding a job?

_____

6 Why do companies break up complex tasks into smaller tasks?

_____

7 What is the Hall of Fame or Shame?

_____

8 Why might turking be suitable for the short term, but not as a career?

_____

_____

F. Read these sentences and choose the best summary for Listening 3.

☐ Crowdsourcing is a way for a company to build up a workforce of dedicated contractors who can help the company address long-term needs in online industries.

☐ Turking is a popular way to earn money in the short term but is legally questionable because of low payments and a lack of benefits for workers.

☐ Anyone can make money online by taking on jobs working for Facebook, Twitter, LinkedIn and other companies that need help with a variety of micro-tasks.

Academic
Survival Skill

We often examine two or more things to compare (find similarities) and contrast (find differences). Planning a compare and contrast presentation sometimes begins with a Venn diagram of overlapping circles. The following example compares and contrasts deep sea divers with astronauts.

A. Add one more item to each part of the Venn diagram.

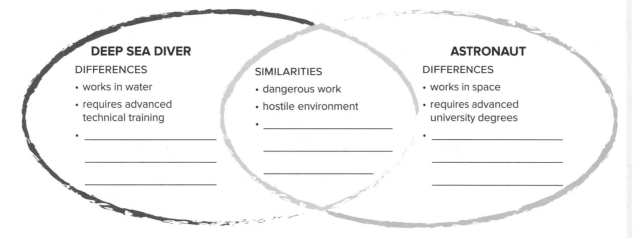

DEEP SEA DIVER

DIFFERENCES

• works in water
• requires advanced technical training
• _____
_____
_____

SIMILARITIES

• dangerous work
• hostile environment
• _____
_____
_____

ASTRONAUT

DIFFERENCES

• works in space
• requires advanced university degrees
• _____
_____
_____

B. Here is an outline for a compare and contrast presentation structure for two speakers. You could also adapt it for one speaker. With a partner, fill in the correct information in the brackets. Use a separate page to write notes on what you would each say. Then, discuss what else you could add.

COMPARE AND CONTRAST PRESENTATION	SPEAKING NOTES
Introduce yourselves and your topic.	Hello. My name is [student A], and this is my partner [student B]. Today, we will be talking about two jobs: [job A] and [job B].
Describe each job. Use the feedback you received on your Warm-Up presentation to deliver a clearer message.	I [student A] will begin by talking about the first job, [A]. Now, let me [student B] continue by talking about the second job, [B].
Introduce what is similar and different. Try to include three points for each. Use compare words and phrases (*in the same way, similarly, likewise*) and contrast words and phrases (*however, on the other hand, but, unlike*). Use what you've learned about comparatives and superlatives to contrast the jobs.	I [student A] will talk about the similarities between [job A] and [job B].
	I [student B] will now talk about the differences between [job A] and [job B].
Add a conclusion. Focus on an observation about the two jobs.	Although the two jobs seem quite different …
Thank your audience. Ask for questions.	Thank you for your attention. We have time for a few questions.

Citing oral sources and referencing

When you give a presentation, mentioning the sources of your information (citing) helps support your argument. It also helps avoid the appearance of plagiarism—taking the ideas of others and presenting them as your own. Besides citing your sources, you need to provide references. When you use text in your presentations, such as a handout or a computer presentation slide, consider including properly formatted references to give appropriate credit.

My eLab
Visit My eLab Documents to review APA formats for citing and referencing original content.

C. With a partner, discuss the following three presentations of similar information. Which one sounds the most convincing? Why?

☐ There's no reason to fear unknown situations. When confronted with the unknown, the most successful people figure out what is it they want.

☐ There's no reason to fear unknown situations. As Paul Brown wrote, "When confronted with the unknown, the most successful people figure out what is it they want."

☐ There's no reason to fear unknown situations. As business author and blogger Paul Brown wrote in *Forbes Magazine* in 2012, "When confronted with the unknown, the most successful people figure out what is it they want."

FINAL ASSIGNMENT
Give a Compare and Contrast Presentation

Use everything you learned in this chapter to prepare and give a presentation that compares and contrasts your perfect job with that of a partner's.

A. With a partner, discuss the perfect jobs you each presented in the Warm-Up Assignment. Find comparisons (similarities) and contrasts (differences) and organize your ideas on a Venn diagram (see Academic Survival Skill).

B. Write an outline of your presentation. Use the compare and contrast presentation structure you learned in Academic Survival Skill. When you compare or contrast your perfect jobs, use comparative and superlative adjectives (review Focus on Grammar, page 30).

C. Practise your presentation. Then, together, present it to the class. When you speak, vary your intonation and stress (see Focus on Speaking, page 36).

D. While you listen to other students' presentations, use the active listening strategies you learned in Focus on Listening (page 26): ask questions and take notes so that you will be prepared to give feedback.

E. Once everyone has presented, ask for feedback from your teacher and classmates on how you could improve your presentation.

Visit My eLab Documents for more tips on giving presentations.

How confident
are you?

Think about what you learned in this chapter. Use the table to decide what you should review.

I LEARNED ...	I AM CONFIDENT	I NEED TO REVIEW
vocabulary related to jobs;	☐	☐
how to use active listening strategies;	☐	☐
when to use comparative and superlative adjectives;	☐	☐
how to use intonation and stress;	☐	☐
how to give a descriptive presentation;	☐	☐
compare and contrast presentation structure;	☐	☐
about citations and references in presentations;	☐	☐
how to give a compare and contrast presentation with a partner.	☐	☐

VOCABULARY
Challenge

Think about the vocabulary and ideas in this chapter. Use these words to write two sentences that summarize new ways of working.

adapt	capacities	consequences	declined	outcome	priorities

_____

_____

_____

_____

_____

My eLab

Visit My eLab to build on what you've learned.

CHAPTER 3

People in Motion

Transportation is one of the most important issues of our time. Not only do more people need to go more places, they are also using a wider range of ways of doing so than ever before. With more people in motion come problems of increased air and noise pollution, and the waste of valuable land and resources. Even for those who work at home, there are still shopping trips to make to buy food and other necessities, and trucks are necessary to stock these stores.

How will you move around your world in the next thirty years?

In this chapter, you will

- learn vocabulary related to transportation;
- learn interviewing skills;
- focus on listening for a purpose;
- review the structure of question types;
- write survey questions;
- conduct an oral survey and present the results.

GEARING UP

A. Look at the pie chart and then answer the questions.

How Philadelphians commute to work

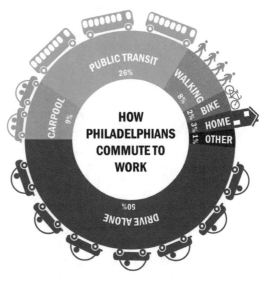

Source: Yamamoto, E. (2014). *How Philadelphians commute to work.* Philadelphia Mayor's Office of Transportation & Utilities (MOTU). Retrieved from http://phillymotu.wordpress.com/tag/commute-mode-split/

❶ The pie chart shows the commuting (travelling to work) choices of people from Philadelphia. Most people drive alone. Why would this be a concern?

_____

❷ What public transit options are common in big cities?

_____

❸ Only 8 percent of Philadelphia's population walk to work. Why do you think this number is so low?

_____

_____

❹ What types of jobs are people likely to have if they work from home?

_____

_____

B. Discuss the questions and your answers, first with a partner, then in a group.

Listening for a Purpose

When you listen, you are listening for detail and gist. Listening for detail is when you want to note one particular bit of information, such as the due date of an assignment. Listening for gist is the opposite; it's about getting a general sense or summary of what is being said. There are, however, other listening strategies.

A. Match each listening strategy to its definition.

LISTEN ...		DEFINITIONS
❶ for attitude and opinion	_____	a) to check for important vocabulary
❷ for comparisons and contrasts	_____	b) to consider the worth of a speaker's ideas
❸ for key words	_____	c) to measure a speaker's true feelings and message
❹ for sequence	_____	d) to consider similarities and differences
❺ to clarify	_____	e) to understand the order of events
❻ to evaluate	_____	f) to understand something complicated

B. Read this excerpt from Listening 3. Then, answer the questions.

> Welcome to the Future Mobility Conference. In this session, Dr. Andrea Parkin will report on a survey that she and her colleagues conducted on the future transportation needs of Vancouver, Canada. The title of her presentation is "Future Perfect: Designing Cities around People."

❶ Which listening strategies could you use when listening to the rest of the lecture? What would you listen for when using each strategy? Discuss your answers in a group.

❷ Think of the type of audience that would be interested in this lecture. What would be their purpose in listening?

_____

_____

_____

_____

❸ What would you want to learn from this lecture? That is, what would be useful to you personally?

_____

_____

_____

_____

C. In this excerpt from Listening 1, Ryan Chin talks about self-driving cars. Use the clarify strategy from task A to highlight key information.

> Well, I think the commercial operators are very focused on manufacturability, cost, reliability and following all the safety rules. Our research is really looking way beyond what the industry is doing. The industry is probably looking between two and five years. Our job is to look way beyond that, five, ten, even further, ahead. We have to look at new trends, what's going to be disruptive in terms of technology and strategy.

A. Below are words and phrases from the Academic Word List that you will find in Listening 1. Highlight the words you understand and then circle the words you use.

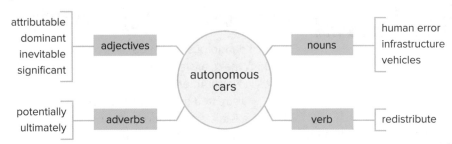

attributable
dominant
inevitable
significant
— **adjectives**

potentially
ultimately
— **adverbs**

autonomous cars

nouns —
human error
infrastructure
vehicles

verb — redistribute

B. Choose the phrase that best completes each sentence. Key words are in bold.

1 All of the transportation problems were **attributable** to _____.
   a) improvements to the highways
   b) breakdowns of the buses
   c) more funds being available

2 The city's **dominant** means of transportation is still _____.
   a) finding ways to work at home
   b) journeys in individual cars
   c) the minor travel options

3 Her mention of **human error** in accidents referred to _____.
   a) barriers such as unsafe sidewalks
   b) physical shortcomings among cyclists
   c) mistakes made by distracted drivers

4 After considering many options, the city **ultimately** _____.
   a) decided to promote carpooling
   b) started to consider discussions
   c) thought about a preliminary report

5 The report uses the term **vehicles** to include _____.
   a) pedestrians, bicycles and cars
   b) cars, cyclists and trucks
   c) cars, buses and trucks

C. Match each word to its definition.

WORDS		DEFINITIONS
❶ inevitable	_____	a) supporting organization of something
❷ infrastructure	_____	b) important
❸ potentially	_____	c) spread something again
❹ redistribute	_____	d) certain to happen
❺ significant	_____	e) having the capacity to develop

LISTENING ❶ Autonomous Cars and the Future of Cities

The most dangerous thing you face on the road is not other cars, but other drivers. Cars don't make mistakes, drivers do—and frequently. Each year, about four million crashes in North America are caused by preoccupied drivers who are tired or distracted by something happening inside or outside the car. Increasingly, mistakes are made by drivers who are focused on their mobile phones, sending or receiving texts and phone calls. Listening 1 introduces autonomous cars—cars that make all the driving decisions on their own—that would eliminate many of these problems.

Before You Listen

A. In a group, discuss reasons why autonomous cars would be a good idea, as well as the problems that could occur with a car that drove itself.

B. A *lidar detector* is a laser detector used to sense other people and vehicles on the road. It uses *algorithms* (mathematical formulae) to estimate distances and speeds and make corrections to the autonomous vehicle's driving. Below are other words to help you understand this listening. Match each word to its definition.

WORDS		DEFINITIONS
❶ congestion	_____	a) promotional excitement
❷ droves	_____	b) insensible from alcohol or drugs
❸ hype	_____	c) many of something, such as people
❹ impaired	_____	d) crowding
❺ platoon	_____	e) people who live in cities
❻ urbanites	_____	f) group of people working together

While You Listen

C. The first time you listen, try to get a general sense of what is being said. Listen a second time and take notes on the arguments for and against autonomous cars. Listen a third time to check your notes.

ARGUMENTS FOR	ARGUMENTS AGAINST
Autonomous cars could reduce car accidents.	*Pollution and congestion are still an issue unless cars go all electric and are shared.*

After You Listen

D. Choose the phrase that best completes each sentence.

1 The City Science Initiative is a network of research groups that looks at _____.

   a) technology in city infrastructures

   b) ways to improve science education

2 Chin and his colleagues at MIT are looking at the big picture of _____.

   a) the screens used to navigate cars

   b) how self-driving cars will help shape cities

3 Autonomous vehicles will get better because of _____.

   a) smart cities with access to sensors and cameras

   b) more efficient batteries and computers

4 The main cost of the vehicles is the lidar detector, which is a set of radars _____.

   a) used to avoid detection by police

   b) that make an image of the surroundings

5 Jim Pisz from Toyota referred to autonomous vehicles as a shiny object, _____.

   a) because the practical benefits are not clear

   b) referring to safety paint designs

6 About two-thirds of all accidents are caused by human error such

as _____.

a) poor road design

b) drinking, texting, telephoning, eating, sleeping

7 The biggest problem with car sharing is _____.

a) drop-offs where there is no demand

b) a lack of interested passengers

8 Private cars are not going to go away but _____.

a) they are likely to become smaller

b) there will be a shift away from private ownership

E. The narrator of Listening 1, Nora Young, says she is skeptical (doubtful) about the idea of autonomous cars. What does she see as the bigger problem? Do you agree? Discuss with a partner.

> Now, I have to admit, I've been a bit of an autonomous car skeptic. Not so much about the technical capability; it just seems like it's directing a lot of resources at improving the individual car, when the problem is actually much bigger: how to move people around in increasingly large megacities with congestion and pollution.

Develop Your Vocabulary: Download and label photographs to help you remember details related to things like autonomous cars.

F. Based on your answers to task C, would you recommend that cities encourage the use of autonomous cars? Why or why not? Discuss in a group.

FOCUS ON GRAMMAR

Indirect and Tag Questions

In Listening 1, Ryan Chin is asked: "Can we talk a bit about what potential autonomous cars have for changing the way we think about how we design and use our cities?" This is an example of an *indirect question*.

Here is the same question, but asked in two different ways.

DIRECT QUESTION: What potential do autonomous cars have for changing the way we think about how we design and use our cities?

Use what you learn about indirect and tag questions when you prepare assignments.

TAG QUESTION: We can talk a bit about what potential autonomous cars have for changing the way we think about how we design and use our cities, can't we?

Indirect questions are commonly used in formal and academic English and are considered more polite than direct questions. They are also used with people you don't know.

INDIRECT QUESTION PHRASE	SUBJECT	MODAL + MAIN VERB	ADDITIONAL INFORMATION
Can you tell me if/whether	you	could lend	me your car?
Do you know if/whether	the pool	might open	at noon?

Sometimes, instead of a question, a polite statement implies the question.

I was wondering if/whether	I	may begin	my test.

Tag questions are most often used to confirm information. Add the "tag" to the end of the statement: a positive tag for a negative statement and a negative tag for a positive statement.

STATEMENT	QUESTION TAG
You're taking the plane,	aren't you?
He isn't taking the train,	is he?
You can lend me your car,	can't you?
She can't lend me her car,	can she?
You ride a bike,	don't you?
We never went on a train,	did we?

A. Complete the table. Fill in the blanks with the correct form of the question. Then, practise asking the questions with a partner.

DIRECT QUESTION	INDIRECT QUESTION OR POLITE STATEMENT	TAG QUESTION
❶ Will you buy an electric car next year?	I was wondering if you might buy an electric car next year.	*You're buying an electric car next year, aren't you?*
❷ _____ _____ _____	_____ _____ _____	We're going to see plug-ins on every corner, aren't we?
❸ Is this car just a rich person's plaything?	_____ _____ _____	_____ _____ _____
❹ _____ _____ _____	Could you tell me if you consider buses comfortable?	_____ _____ _____
❺ _____ _____ _____	_____ _____ _____	You can't tell me the practical benefits of bicycles, can you?
❻ Can we talk about autonomous cars?	_____ _____ _____	_____ _____ _____

A. Below are words and phrases from the Academic Word List that you will find in Listening 2. Highlight the words you understand and then circle the words you use.

committed
convincing
fundamental
geopolitical

adjectives

electric cars

nouns — range anxiety
sequel

verb — concluded
convert

B. Fill in the blanks with the words that have the closest meaning to the phrases in bold.

convert	convincing	fundamental	sequel

1. **Making our beliefs acceptable to** (_____) her involved listing all the facts.

2. This **continuation of the story** (_____) was released two years after the first movie.

3. A **basic and well-known** (_____) law while driving is the need to stop for pedestrians.

4. They wanted to **change to an alternative** (_____) form of energy for their home.

C. Highlight the best definition for each word or phrase. Use a dictionary to check your answers.

1. geopolitical a) about territory and government b) about mining and government

2. committed a) lost forever b) tied to a plan

3. range anxiety a) worried about going too far b) fear of a burning stove

4. concluded a) started b) finished

D. VOCABULARY EXTENSION: The word *geopolitical* is made up of the prefix *geo-* (the Greek prefix for Earth) and *political* (the governmental affairs of a country). Add two more examples for each prefix.

PREFIX	MEANING	EXAMPLES
1. geo-	Earth	geography, _____
2. extra-	additional	extraordinary, _____
3. micro-	small	microscope, _____
4. non-	not	non-violent, _____
5. sub-	under	subdivision, _____

Plugging in: The Future of Electric Cars

Electric cars are not new. The first ones were invented in the early 1800s, and in the early 1900s, they competed with gasoline-powered cars. But because of limited battery life, electric cars were mostly suited to short trips within cities. As roads expanded, gasoline-powered cars were better suited to long distances. Now, better batteries, more charging stations and better car designs are making non-polluting electric cars an alternative to gasoline-powered cars. Listening 2 is a portion of a documentary about the return of electric cars.

Before You Listen

A. Compare electric and gasoline-powered cars. List what you think are the advantages and the disadvantages of each. Discuss with a partner.

	ADVANTAGES	DISADVANTAGES
ELECTRIC CARS		
GASOLINE-POWERED CARS		

B. Read the introduction to Listening 2. It talks about a "tipping point" (when small changes grow to make a large change). What small changes could now make electric vehicles a more attractive option? Would you want to drive one? Why or why not? Discuss in a group.

> **NARRATOR:** Chris Payne will tell you appetite is growing for electric cars.
>
> **CHRIS PAYNE:** We're in the tipping point now.
>
> **NARRATOR:** He's best known as director of the biting documentary *Who Killed the Electric Car?*
>
> **CP:** I wasn't really a car guy ever, but I was really into cool technology.
>
> **NARRATOR:** Back in the 90s, he drove a General Motors EV1: the first mass-market electric car. It held the promise of an oil-free future, but GM concluded it was losing money on the EV1 and destroyed them all. Chris Payne was incensed [angry].

C. These words and expressions are used in Listening 2. Working with a partner, write the meaning of each one. Guess at those you don't know. Then, while you listen, check your meanings.

WORDS/EXPRESSIONS	MEANINGS
1 circuit board	*electronics that control the flow of electricity*
2 chronicled	
3 smidge	
4 zero emissions	
5 internal combustion engine	
6 begging the question	*raising a question about something*
7 money where your mouth is	*acting according to your opinions*
8 petroleum products	
9 holy warriors	*people who promote a cause in an extreme way*

While You Listen

D. Follow Listening 2. Use the outline format from Chapter 1 (p. 10), to write key points.

Chris Payne	• director of *Who Killed the Electric Car?* _____
EV1	• few left/most _____ • Payne _____
Payne has _____ electric cars.	• the cars use _____ • don't require _____ • he wants every car _____

Elon Musk's Tesla S1	• Car of the year
	• 0–100 km in about _____
	• benefits
	  – a guilt-free _____
	  – zero _____
	  – storage space _____
	• cost _____
	  – wealth = _____
	  _____

John O'Dell: unlike electric cars	• gas cars easy to find _____
	• can be _____ everywhere
	• marketing must overcome the _____
	_____
gasoline engines	• will remain popular _____
	• unless _____
fear of change disappears	• once someone _____
	• they become like holy warriors (enthusiastic converts)

After You Listen

E. Indicate whether these statements are true or false, according to the listening.

STATEMENTS	TRUE	FALSE
1 General Motors destroyed all its EV1 electric cars because they were unprofitable.	☐	☐
2 The Volt, Leaf and Tesla S1 are all examples of gas-electric hybrids.	☐	☐
3 The Tesla car's benefits include more storage room and fast speeds.	☐	☐
4 The cost of a Tesla sports car is about $50,000.	☐	☐
5 Maggie Argirio feels buying an electric car avoids social responsibility.	☐	☐
6 The fact that "car reviewers were raving" means reviewers were greatly impressed.	☐	☐
7 The expression *valley of death* refers to a range limit in kilometres.	☐	☐
8 The expression *holy warrior* suggests you will like electric cars once you try one.	☐	☐

F. Answer these questions.

1 From what you now understand from Listening 2, which factors have led to the tipping point in favour of electric cars?

_____

_____

2 What comparison is being made when one of the speakers refers to guilt-free sports cars?

_____

_____

③ How does buying a $100,000 sports car "help the technology forward"?

_____

_____

Pronunciation: In words like "listen," the "t" is not pronounced. In conversation, it might not be pronounced in phrases such as "don't buy apples."

④ The valley of death refers to a point between when the first people adopt a new technology and when that technology finally becomes popular with the general public. What allows a technology to escape the valley of death?

_____

_____

FOCUS ON SPEAKING

Learning Interviewing Skills

Interviewing is a basic and important form of academic research. When you conduct an interview, you ask prepared questions and sometimes follow up with new questions based on the interviewee's replies. Interview questions often start with *who, what, when, where, why* and *how*. But don't ask questions to which you already know the answers. For example, if you were interviewing your city's mayor about a new transit plan, the *who* and *what* questions might be unnecessary.

A. Which questions would you ask if you wanted to know the routes and means of transportation students take from home to class? Write three questions and ask six students to respond. Write your questions and their answers on a separate page.

B. Follow-up questions develop an interviewee's answers into other questions. Ask students you interviewed follow-up questions to collect additional information.

Why do you travel by _____ and not by _____?

What difference does the weather make to the route you travel?

Closed-ended questions invite one-word answers such as *yes* or *no*.
Open-ended questions and clarification statements require longer answers.

C. Discuss a current news story with a partner. Use these phrases to find out more information. Take turns being the interviewer and the interviewee.

- Can you think of another way/time/method to ...?
- Could you describe/explain/outline ...?
- Tell me about ...
- What do you think would happen/change/improve if ...?
- What else is important/significant about ...?
- What should someone know if ...?

D. Change these closed-ended questions to open-ended questions or clarification statements. Use expressions you learned in task C. Practise asking and answering the open-ended questions with a partner.

CLOSED-ENDED QUESTIONS	OPEN-ENDED QUESTIONS/CLARIFICATION STATEMENTS
❶ Do you go to university?	Tell me about *your education.* _____
❷ Do you take the bus to school?	_____ _____ _____
❸ Do you use a bicycle?	What are your attitudes toward _____ _____ _____
❹ Is the bus a good way to travel?	_____ _____ _____
❺ Do you ever take a taxi?	What has been your experience _____ _____ _____
❻ Have you ever walked to school?	When is walking _____ _____ _____

Academic
Survival Skill

Creating Survey Questions

A survey is a convenient way to collect information from a group of people. Start by considering what information—or data—you want to have and the target group that can give it to you. For example, you might be interested in what students' transportation choices might be if a public transportation strike stopped bus and subway services.

A. Indicate which of these would be good questions to ask in a survey. Discuss with a partner. Improve the questions that are vague or unrealistic. Use what you learned about open-ended questions in Focus on Speaking.

POTENTIAL SURVEY QUESTIONS	YES	NO
1 Could you tell me if you take the bus to school?	☐	☐
2 What kind of transportation do you take to school?	☐	☐
3 You can share a car to get to school, can't you?	☐	☐
4 How far is it between your home and school?	☐	☐
5 Can you explain what would make your trip to school better?	☐	☐
6 You work on your laptop on your way to school, don't you?	☐	☐
7 If you were in a wheelchair, how would you get to school?	☐	☐
8 Can I ask if you might walk five miles to school to save money?	☐	☐
9 Do you know if you might spend $30 a day on transportation to school?	☐	☐
10 Do you prefer taking a bus or riding a bicycle to school?	☐	☐

B. Some survey questions offer more than one choice. Add four more options to this question.

If price was not a concern, would you go to school by …?

☐ bicycle ☐ individual car ☐ _____ ☐ _____

☐ bus ☐ taxi ☐ _____ ☐ _____

C. Practise asking and answering the questions in tasks A and B with a partner.

WARM-UP ASSIGNMENT
Conduct an Oral Survey

Use what you learned in Academic Survival Skill and Focus on Speaking to write survey questions about transportation choices students would make during an emergency, such as a natural disaster (e.g., earthquake, flood, severe storm).

A. Consider the type of information, or data, on transportation choices you wish to get from other students. Write an outline with the questions you want answered.

B. Write two types of questions:
- four indirect questions (see Focus on Grammar, page 50)
- one check box question with six choices

Test your questions with a partner and review the language to make sure it is correct and easy to understand.

C. Conduct your questionnaire by asking six or more students for their answers. For the indirect questions, take notes on the students' responses. Ask follow-up questions for clarification.

D. Collect and summarize your data. You will use this data in the Final Assignment presentation.

VOCABULARY BUILD 3

A. Below are words from the Academic Word List that you will find in Listening 3. Highlight the words you understand and then circle the words you use.

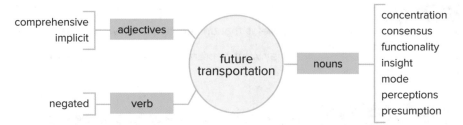

comprehensive
implicit — **adjectives**

future transportation — **nouns** —
concentration
consensus
functionality
insight
mode
perceptions
presumption

negated — **verb**

B. Choose the phrase that best completes each sentence. Key words are in bold.

1 Their plans for the performance were **negated** by _____.
   a) the audience patiently waiting
   b) the loud fire alarm going off
   c) the peaceful setting in the forest

2 The chess players complained that their **concentration** was

_____.

   a) interrupted by the constant ringing of phones
   b) more enjoyable because of the audience talking
   c) based on one part juice to two hundred parts water

3 Their **perceptions** of the traffic jam were influenced by _____.

   a) their enjoyment of the movie they were watching at home

   b) the smooth flow of their and others' cars on the highway

   c) the fact they could see the terrible accident ahead of them

4 There was a **presumption** that each of the company's partners _____.

   a) felt it was their duty to think of themselves

   b) were not paid for any of the work they did

   c) were working for the good of the company

5 The plan was extremely **comprehensive** because _____.

   a) they had thought of every detail

   b) the team put it together in ten minutes

   c) it didn't matter if it worked or not

C. Fill in the blanks with the correct words to complete the paragraph. Use a dictionary for words you don't understand.

consensus	functionality	implicit	insight	mode

A common _____ among university professors is that the

_____ of what they teach is usually second to the theories

they explore. This is reflected in the _____ of instruction,

teaching students to reflect on example after example in hopes that at least

one new _____ will develop. The _____

belief is that universities don't want to train students to do yesterday's jobs;

they want to prepare them to meet tomorrow's challenges.

My eLab

Visit My eLab to complete Vocabulary Review exercises for this chapter.

LISTENING ③   Future Perfect: The Future Mobility Conference

Since the invention of cars in the nineteenth century, private car ownership has steadily increased. In 2013, more than eighty-seven million cars were produced,

adding to hundreds of millions already on the world's roads. But today, many young people are looking for alternatives. They object to the car's financial costs, as well as to its environmental costs, both in the use of materials involved in making the car and the pollution resulting from running it. There are many transportation alternatives and new ones are likely to be invented in coming years. Listening 3 reports on the findings of a survey that was conducted to find out what students thought about the future of transportation in the city.

Before You Listen

A. In a group, discuss what you think are the future mobility (transportation) options for you over the next thirty years.

B. In the introduction to Listening 3, Dr. Parkin shares an anecdote (a story with a message) about Henry Ford. What is the anecdote's message and how does it relate to future transportation choices?

> Our work in this area began with a quote attributed to automobile pioneer Henry Ford: "If I had asked people what they wanted, they would have said faster horses."

_____

_____

_____

C. These words will help you understand Listening 3. Highlight the best definition for each. Use a dictionary to look up those words that are unfamiliar.

1. obstacle   a) playground feature   b) something in the way

2. dedicated   a) always resourceful   b) meant for a specific purpose

3. intriguing   a) interesting   b) digging deeper

4. constituted   a) officially documented   b) made up of

5. elicit   a) ask for   b) give up

While You Listen

D. Use the listening strategies you learned in Focus on Listening (p. 46), and the key words in the table to take notes on the information in the report. Pay particular attention to the numbers that are mentioned.

LISTENING STRATEGIES	NOTES
LISTEN FOR KEY WORDS • survey, future transportation, Vancouver, Canada, title	_survey @ future transportation needs; title_ Future Perfect: Designing Cities around People
• Dr. Andrea Parkin, quote, marketing, imagination	
LISTEN FOR ATTITUDE AND OPINION • target audience	

LISTENING STRATEGIES	NOTES
LISTEN FOR COMPARISONS AND CONTRASTS • Vancouver, transportation options	
• survey, transportation options, private cars, freedom, benefits, • cycling and public transit	
LISTEN TO EVALUATE • survey question, answers • another question, pollution	
• survey questions, proposals, protection	
• functionality to bus stops, examples, why students don't want Wi-Fi	
LISTEN FOR ATTITUDE AND OPINION • bicycles, physical safety, dedicated bicycle, divided, post-survey interviews	
LISTEN FOR COMPARISONS AND CONTRASTS • awareness and attitudes, solutions Copenhagen, Vancouver, rain, temperatures, sunshine, flat/hills	
LISTEN TO EVALUATE • Vancouver future	

❗ *After you listen, write out your notes while you remember the details.*

After You Listen

E. Review your notes and write the significance of each number mentioned in the report.

1 thirty years: *Number of years students are likely to be using different kinds of transportation for a variety of purposes, including commuting to work.*

2 twelve students: _____

_____

3 328: _____

_____

4 291 students/89 percent: _____

_____

5 53 percent: _____

_____

6 23 percent: _____

_____

7 18 percent: _____

_____

8 59 out of 328 students: _____

_____

9 61 percent: _____

_____

10 50/50 percent: _____

_____

11 36 percent: _____

_____

12 1.8 percent: _____

_____

13 152 metres: _____

_____

F. Answer these questions.

1 Why did Dr. Parkin survey university students instead of working adults?

_____

_____

2 Why did students identify transportation by private cars as important?

_____

_____

3 Why are many students uninterested in having Wi-Fi at bus stops and on buses?

_____

_____

4 The idea of students taking personal helicopters is a joke, but why does Dr. Parkin mention it?

_____

_____

5 What is the reason for comparing Vancouver to Copenhagen?

_____

_____

FINAL ASSIGNMENT
Prepare and Present an Oral Survey

Use what you learned in this chapter to prepare and present the results of the survey you conducted in the Warm-Up Assignment.

A. Review your data from the Warm-Up Assignment. You may want to survey additional students. Convert all figures into statistics.

B. Structure your presentation. Use this format to write notes on a separate page.

PRESENTATION STRUCTURE	NOTES
Greet the audience: introduce yourself and the reason for your survey. Explain the problem(s) or question(s) that led to the research. This raises audience interest.	Good morning/afternoon. My name is … and today I will be talking about … The question/problem that led to my research was …
Identify your objectives. Describe the target group you chose, what kind of information you wanted to get, and why this target group was the best choice.	In this survey, I questioned (number) university students to determine how they would respond to (the topic). I chose this target group because …
Explain your data collection process. Review the steps you took in preparing and conducting your survey, including how your questions matched your objectives.	My questions for the survey included … The first question addressed the objective ….
Describe your findings. Briefly mention any data that seemed routine, expected or inconclusive, and focus on surprising findings.	As expected, (the target group) felt … and …, although there were some surprising findings. First, …
Summarize your findings and make recommendations. Summarize the main point of your findings. If appropriate, give recommendations.	In summary, the data suggests … Based on what I have learned from the results of my survey, … should consider …

C. Practise your presentation on your own, and then with a partner. Avoid reading from your notes. If you need notes, write key facts and figures on a single small card.

D. Give your presentation.

E. While other students present their reports, take notes using the listening strategies you learned in Focus on Listening, on page 46. If you need additional information, or clarification, ask questions at the end of each presentation (refer to Focus on Grammar, page 50). Be prepared to answer questions on your presentation.

F. After, ask your teacher and other students for feedback to help you improve your presentation style.

My eLab

Visit My eLab Documents for more help with giving presentations.

How confident
are you?

Think about what you learned in this chapter. Use the table to decide what you should review.

I LEARNED ...	I AM CONFIDENT	I NEED TO REVIEW
vocabulary related to transportation;	☐	☐
interviewing skills;	☐	☐
how to listen for a purpose;	☐	☐
the structure of question types;	☐	☐
how to write survey questions;	☐	☐
how to conduct an oral survey and present the results.	☐	☐

VOCABULARY
Challenge

Think about the vocabulary and ideas in this chapter. Use these words to write two sentences that summarize the future of transportation.

concluded	convincing	inevitable	insight	perceptions	significant

_____

_____

_____

_____

_____

My eLab

Visit My eLab to build on what you learned.

CHAPTER 4

Building a Better Brain

A common myth is that we use only 10 percent of our brain. In fact, we use it all and can accomplish extraordinary things. For example, while reading these words, you process the shapes of letters and hear sounds and explore meaning. You compare new information to what you know already, store that information in short-term memory and then make decisions about whether or not you agree with it. At the same time, you are conscious of the sounds, sights and smells that surround you, the physical sensations you feel as well as various ideas and memories. But how is all this possible? Despite being studied for centuries, the brain has not yet revealed all of its secrets.

What would you like to understand about your brain?

In this chapter,
you will

- learn vocabulary related to mental and emotional health;
- listen to infer meaning from context;

- learn how to keep a listener's attention;
- review the simple past and present perfect tenses;

- learn how to prepare an academic presentation;
- give an academic presentation.

GEARING UP

A. Look at the pie chart and then answer the questions.

Preferences of what 18–34 year-olds would most like to be

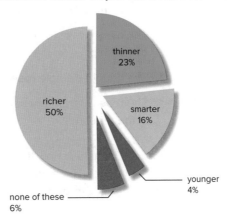

Source: Harris Interactive. (2010, August 26). *Would Americans Rather Be Younger, Thinner, Richer or Smarter?* Retrieved from http://www.harrisinteractive.com/NewsRoom/HarrisPolls/tabid/447/ctl/ReadCustom%20Default/ mid/1508/ArticleId/555/Default.aspx

1 Why might this age group's highest preference be wanting to be richer?

_____

_____

2 Why might happiness be related to being thinner?

_____

_____

3 Why might being smarter be a relatively minor preference?

_____

_____

4 Which of the preferences could most likely help achieve the other ones?

_____

_____

B. Discuss the questions and your answers, first with a partner, then in a group.

Inferring Meaning from Context

The meaning of a word or phrase depends on the context. For example, consider the meaning of the word *right* in these sentences:

It's on your **right**. (direction)
Education is a **right**. (a moral or legal privilege)
The answer is **right**. (correct)
We can stop **right** here. (exactly)

Some words can have opposite meanings, depending on the context.

A. Write the meaning of the word in bold in each sentence.

MEANING

❶ I'm going to **bill** (v.) her for the damage
to my car.   _____

❷ I paid a **bill** (n.) for the damage to her car.   _____

❸ He will **hold** (v.) your package.   _____

❹ The cargo was stored in the **hold** (n.)
of the ship.   _____

❺ She bought a single **rose** (n.) at the market. _____

❻ She **rose** (v.) from her seat to talk
at the meeting.   _____

The above examples show that it is important to understand the many meanings of common words. But if you hear an unusual word, you can use one of these context strategies to guess its meaning.

CONTEXT STRATEGIES	EXAMPLE
CONTRAST: Listen for words that indicate a contrast (*but, unlike*) between one word or phrase and others in the sentence that you might understand.	**Brainstorming**, unlike remembering, is related to the future.
DEFINITION: Listen for words or phrases that signal a definition (*X is, like, a Y*) that are included in the sentence.	**Brainstorming** is a process of putting together ideas.
EXAMPLE: Listen for words or phrases that refer to an example (*such as, for example*).	A **brainstorming** activity, such as asking people to share ideas in turns, is a good icebreaker.
GRAMMAR: Try to determine the part of speech (noun, verb, adjective, adverb). This will help you understand the word's relationship to other words.	**Brainstorming** can involve sticking ideas on a wall in categories.
LOGIC: Use what you understand about the rest of the sentence to infer the meaning of the key word.	To engage in **brainstorming**, all you need is a group of people and a problem.
ROOT WORD AND/OR COMPOUND WORD: Listen for parts of the word that are similar to other words that you know (*brain + storm*).	The word ***brainstorming*** refers to a process of discussing spontaneous ideas.

B. Write the meaning of each word in bold. Then, write the strategy you used to help you understand the word. Check the meanings in the dictionary.

		MEANINGS	STRATEGIES
❶	The former millionaire maintained his **dignity** despite losing all his money.		
❷	Georgia showed **aptitude** for running, and the other girls couldn't keep up.		
❸	Your **spouse**—by which I mean your husband or wife—must also attend the meeting.		
❹	He was **intimidated** by the amount of work, feeling it was too much for him to do.		
❺	There are six **neurologists** studying her brain activity.		
❻	With no **ego**, you would not care about yourself or what others thought about you.		

VOCABULARY BUILD 1

A. Below are words from the Academic Word List that you will find in Listening 1. Highlight the words you understand and then circle the words you use.

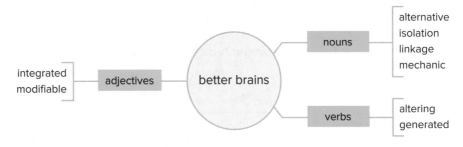

B. Match each word to its definition.

WORDS		DEFINITIONS
❶ altering	_____	a) different choice
❷ alternative	_____	b) someone who repairs machines
❸ integrated	_____	c) changing
❹ mechanic	_____	d) fit within something else

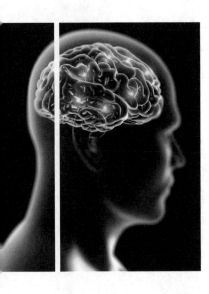

C. Highlight the words that have the closest meaning to the words in bold.

1 The computer **generated** a report on the electrical changes in the patient's brain.

    a) invented   b) deleted   c) created

2 The **isolation** of the coastal village meant it depended on supplies from ships.

    a) closeness   b) remoteness   c) nearness

3 The **linkage** between industry and certain kinds of pollution has been proven.

    a) distraction   b) connection   c) infection

4 Computers that are **modifiable** can be used for much longer.

    a) outdated   b) futuristic   c) adaptable

LISTENING ❶   Better Brains

Of all the organs in our body, our brain is the most complex. The brain includes approximately one hundred billion nerve cells—called *neurons*—each linked to thousands of others via *synapses*. It seems reasonable to take care of such an important organ. Proper diet, physical and mental exercises, and wearing protective gear, like helmets, are some of the ways we can maintain our brain health. Mental exercises, in particular, build and strengthen neural pathways and connections in our brains. In Listening 1, neuroscientist Richard Restak talks to writer Susan Orlean about our brain's potential.

Before You Listen

A. The Greek scientist Aristotle (384–322 BCE) believed that the heart was the centre of feelings and movement and that the brain was simply for cooling the blood. Without our modern understanding of the brain, how could you have convinced Aristotle that he was wrong?

_____

_____

_____

B. Look at this diagram of brain functions. Some people believe their strongest skills tend to focus on their left brain or right brain. Do you feel your skills reflect strengths on one side or the other? Discuss in a group.

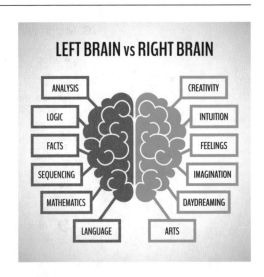

LEFT BRAIN vs RIGHT BRAIN

ANALYSIS   CREATIVITY
LOGIC   INTUITION
FACTS   FEELINGS
SEQUENCING   IMAGINATION
MATHEMATICS   DAYDREAMING
LANGUAGE   ARTS

C. *Strabismus* refers to the eyes not lining up in a way that affects one's focus. *Synthesized* refers to two things brought together to make something new. *Perfect pitch* is the ability to recognize and play musical notes perfectly. Of these three terms, which would you be most and least likely to remember? Why?

_____

_____

_____

While You Listen

D. The first time you listen, try to understand the main idea. Use the strategies you learned in Focus on Listening (page 68) to help you with the meaning of any new vocabulary. Listen a second time and use the timeline to take notes. Write what happens at each stage of development. Listen a third time to review your notes and add details.

AGE	NOTES ON HUMAN DEVELOPMENT
before birth	*maximum number of brain cells*
after birth to 3 months	
7 months to 2 years old	
7 years old	
puberty for girls (10 to 14)	
girls 11 years old	
puberty for boys (12 to 16)	
boys 15 years old	
early adulthood	
adulthood	
87 years old	

After You Listen

E. Answer these questions.

1. What comparison does Richard Restak make between the brain and a car?

_____

_____

2. What does Restak say about the brains of animals within rich environments?

_____

_____

3. What comparison is Restak making between numbers thrown around in Washington in dollars (billions for budgets) and brain cells?

_____

_____

4. What does Restak feel is the saddest thing about people with Alzheimer's?

_____

_____

5. What is Restak's comparison between the growth of a young child's brain and body?

_____

_____

F. Restak refers to several examples of research on the brain. What is significant about his mention of the following?

1. kittens: _____

_____

_____

2. songbirds: _____

_____

_____

3. monkeys: _____

_____

_____

4. people using canes: _____

_____

Simple Past and Present Perfect Tenses

Both the simple past and the present perfect tenses are used to explain things that have happened. The difference between the two is that the *simple past* describes actions or events that are not connected to the present, whereas the *present perfect* describes actions that started in the past and are either still happening or are otherwise connected to the present in some way. Consider this sentence from Listening 2.

> You actually go through the neuroscience around how our brains have evolved.

In this sentence, it's considered that something happened in the past (our brains evolving) but that the time of that evolution is vague.

Use the simple past or the present perfect tense to describe actions or events in terms of duration, information and time.

	SIMPLE PAST (infinitive + -ed)	PRESENT PERFECT (have/has + past participle)
DURATION	I **talked** with my friends **during free period**. (completed action)	I **have talked** with my friends during free period **today**. (started in the past, connected to the present)
INFORMATION	He **slipped** at the pool and broke his arm. (action happened earlier)	He **has just slipped** at the pool and broke his arm. (action just happened)
TIME	He saw a doctor **at 3:00 p.m.** (time is specific)	He **has seen** a doctor **this afternoon**. (time is vague)

A. Indicate whether these signal words or phrases are used with the simple past or with the present perfect.

SIGNAL WORDS/PHRASES	SIMPLE PAST	PRESENT PERFECT
❶ three years ago	☐	☐
❷ not yet	☐	☐
❸ already	☐	☐
❹ ever	☐	☐
❺ in 2014	☐	☐
❻ just	☐	☐
❼ last night	☐	☐
❽ the other day	☐	☐
❾ until now	☐	☐
❿ up to now	☐	☐
⓫ yesterday	☐	☐

My eLab

Visit My eLab Documents to see the Irregular Verbs List, which shows the simple past and past participles.

B. Change these sentences from the simple past to the present perfect.

1 They picked several kilos of apples.

_____

_____

2 We reduced the number of hours we spent playing chess.

_____

_____

3 She bumped into the table in the library.

_____

_____

4 We looked at the dictionaries in the bookshop window.

_____

_____

5 The committee funded the construction of a new swimming pool.

_____

_____

> ❗ *Use what you learned about the simple past and the present perfect tenses when you prepare assignments.*

6 I called her phone number and left a message.

_____

_____

A. Below are words and phrases from the Academic Word List that you will find in Listening 2. Highlight the words you understand and then circle the words you use.

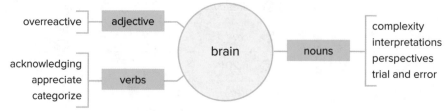

B. Highlight the word or phrase in parentheses that best completes each sentence. Key words are in bold.

1 They decided to (figure out / ignore) the problem through **trial and error**.

2 Several **interpretations** of what caused the accident meant (everyone / no one) agreed.

③ Having several **perspectives** on a problem lets you see it (less / more) clearly.

④ Mother bears with cubs are **overreactive** when there is (quiet / noise) nearby.

C. Fill in the blanks with the correct words to complete the paragraph.

acknowledging	appreciate	categorize	complexity

We can imagine the _____ of the brain by considering how many things it is able to do at the same time. For example, while walking and talking, we can _____ a beautiful sunset. Even something as simple as _____ a greeting requires listening, thinking and the production of a suitable facial expression and reply. Although we can _____ these different actions and even have computers and robots imitate some, it's nearly impossible to imagine a machine that will someday function as well as the human brain.

D. VOCABULARY EXTENSION: Use synonyms to avoid repeating the same word, but be aware that synonyms may have subtle differences in meaning. Look at these synonyms for *complexity* and write definitions.

① complication: _____

_____

② convolution: _____

_____

③ difficulty: _____

_____

④ intricacy: _____

_____

LISTENING ❷   ## Ted Cadsby—Interview with Amanda Lang

Someone from 150 years ago would be overwhelmed by the communications technology—radio, TV, colour photographs, telephones and computers—that we now take for granted. But perhaps we are also overwhelmed, and perhaps our brains are finding it increasingly difficult to process new information from new technologies and make sensible decisions. In Listening 2, author Ted Cadsby suggests that we are lazy thinkers and need to change or face serious consequences.

Before You Listen

A. An important concept in Listening 2 is *linear thinking*. It's often contrasted with *non-linear* or *lateral thinking*. Linear thinking is described as finding an answer by digging a hole deeper; lateral thinking is described as digging several small holes in different places. Indicate which of the following decisions would be more suited to linear thinking and which to lateral thinking. Discuss your choices with a partner.

DECISIONS	LINEAR THINKING	LATERAL THINKING
1 whether or not to buy a bicycle	☐	☐
2 what kind of a bicycle to buy	☐	☐
3 who to vote for	☐	☐
4 whether you will vote	☐	☐

B. Read this excerpt from Listening 2. In it, Cadsby defines what he sees as a mind gap. Write examples of where intuition (making decisions without clear reasons) may get you in trouble. Discuss with a partner.

> It is the gap between our routine way of thinking about things and the way complex world and complex problems work. So the routine default way that we think about everything is fairly straightforward and it works for us most of the time. But when we confront complexity in interpersonal relationships, public policy, business strategy, you name it, there's a gap between our intuitions and how that form of reality actually works.

C. These words and phrases will help you understand Listening 2. Match each word or phrase to its definition.

WORDS/PHRASE		DEFINITIONS
1 cognitive science	_____	a) steep face of a cliff; dangerous situation
2 innumerate	_____	b) extremely and seriously
3 intricate	_____	c) ahead of something's proper time
4 linear	_____	d) basis of an argument
5 precipice	_____	e) complicated or detailed
6 prematurely	_____	f) without basic knowledge of mathematics
7 premise	_____	g) progressing in a series of steps
8 profoundly	_____	h) study of how learning takes place

While You Listen

D. Listening 2 takes the form of an interview. Read the questions and try to predict the answers. The first time you listen, try to get the gist. Notice the use of the simple past and the present perfect verb tenses. Listen a second time and take notes on Cadsby's answers. Listen a third time to add details.

AMANDA LANG'S QUESTIONS	TED CADSBY'S ANSWERS
You actually go through the neuroscience around how our brains have evolved. They stopped evolving—about one thousand years ago? Five hundred years ago?	
And one of the things you point out is that that old linear model that works so well, and it still works well in certain situations, doesn't apply well to real complexity.	Exactly.
Is the first step of this actually acknowledging that to ourselves, that we're not as smart as we think, that we're over confident about our decisions, that we actually need to stop and think about how we think?	We're over-emotional, over-logical, innumerate …
So … linear simplification and the speed … is great, but what are some of the strategies you would have people use to … deal better with the complexity?	one: two:
This kind of thinking … we have a tendency to accept that [believing politicians] more readily. How hard is it to change that?	We need to take more responsibility as an electorate; we can't blame politicians …
This is going to sound a little science fiction but … will we be able to just create things that will do this work for us and we can stay linear and simple?	
So finally, that's a pretty interesting point. We live in a world where things are getting faster and faster … Would you say that actually learning to slow it down is the answer?	Yes, one challenge is …

After You Listen

E. Indicate whether these statements are true or false, according to the listening.

STATEMENTS	TRUE	FALSE
❶ Cadsby believes that people are getting smarter about making decisions.	☐	☐
❷ Cadsby feels there's a gap between thinking about routine things and complex ones.	☐	☐
❸ Doctors washing their hands before an operation is an example of how we are improving our thinking.	☐	☐
❹ Cadsby says that we already spend a lot of time considering how we think.	☐	☐
❺ By linear thinking, Cadsby suggests that we often think in steps, such as by considering cause and effect.	☐	☐
❻ Cadsby believes that computers will soon be able to make many of our decisions.	☐	☐
❼ Cadsby believes we should learn to slow down our thinking processes and get different perspectives.	☐	☐
❽ Cadsby uses a Twitter feed as an example of how we can best manage information.	☐	☐

F. Highlight the word or phrase in parentheses that best completes each sentence. Review your notes if you don't know the answer.

❶ Amanda Lang begins the interview by raising the idea that most of us are (smart / lazy) thinkers.

❷ Lang suggests that a linear model of thinking (still works / doesn't work) in most situations.

❸ One of the concerns is that our brains are the same but our (society / thinking) has changed.

❹ Lang raises the idea that our brains have stopped (evolving / shrinking).

❺ Lang suggests that it's important to acknowledge that we're not as smart as (universities / we) think.

❻ Lang suggests politicians take advantage of our desire to have them (simplify / complicate) issues.

❼ Lang mentions science fiction in the context of using (artificial intelligence / robots) to make better decisions for us.

❽ Lang's mention of things getting faster and faster probably relates to modern (transportation / communication).

FOCUS ON SPEAKING

Keeping a Listener's Attention

One challenge when speaking is finding ways to keep a listener's attention. Body language and eye contact can help, but vocabulary choices and varied sentences make a bigger difference. This starts with avoiding bland words—words that are so common people ignore them. For example, the word *nice* is so overused that it has lost its meaning. Instead, use emotional words—words that stir feelings and evoke associations. For example, *agreeable, wonderful* and *amusing* are synonyms for *nice*, but can have more of an impact.

▶

A. Highlight the emotional word in each pair of synonyms. Then add an emotional synonym of your own.

1. heartbreaking   bad   _____
2. gorgeous   pretty   _____
3. big   enormous   _____
4. respectable   good   _____
5. great   tremendous   _____
6. fascinating   interesting   _____
7. said   suggested   _____

Develop Your Vocabulary: Use a thesaurus to learn new synonyms but check to see they are the same part of speech and have the same meaning.

Varying the length of your sentences adds interest by breaking up the singsong pattern found when you say several sentences with the same number of words.

B. Consider these two paragraphs. The first has sentences of equal lengths; the second varies sentence length. Read them aloud. Which sounds better?

PARAGRAPH 1	PARAGRAPH 2
So, I would like to ask each of you to do one simple non-ape thing. This thing is to make friends outside your group, outside your normal troop of apes. Make friends and say hello to a student sitting alone and invite this student today.	So, I'd like to ask each of you to do one simple non-ape thing. This is it: make friends outside your group, outside your normal troop of apes. Make friends and say hello to a student sitting alone. Invite this student today.

C. Rewrite these sentences into two or more of varying length. Replace bland words with emotional ones. Practise saying the sentences with a partner.

1. You can be a good athlete if you work hard every day and get good food and a lot of sleep.

   You can be a spectacular athlete. You just need to push yourself to the limit.

   Eat hearty food and reward yourself with a good night's rest.

2. Keeping your mind fit is also important because when you think well, you can make good decisions.

   _____

   _____

3. Being physically and mentally fit also improves your moods, which can go from good to bad, particularly among teenagers.

   _____

   _____

4. A helpful strategy is to find like-minded friends who share interests and activities and who can give you positive feedback.

   _____

   _____

Giving Academic Presentations

Throughout your education, you have probably heard many academic presentations. Each presentation had a particular purpose: to inform, to inspire or to persuade. The structure of an academic presentation is similar to that of a paragraph or an essay, with an introduction, supporting information and a conclusion.

Introduction

An introduction to an academic presentation gives reasons for listening. Your introduction might explain the expertise of the speaker so listeners are confident they will learn something new.

Use a phrase to signal that this is an introduction. → Before we begin, let me briefly introduce myself. My name is Dr. Sylvia Chen. I am an anthropologist by training and my research focuses on the lives of university students. ← Give your name, your qualifications or experience or your interest in the topic.

The introduction can also be used to make the purpose of the presentation clear. You can mention three or more points that will be developed later and framed in such a way as to convey intent. Consider these examples.

TO INFORM: Many people don't know about the work of Cambridge mathematician Alan Turing. He was an expert in cryptography, computing and artificial intelligence.

TO INSPIRE: The short life of Anne Frank provides many lessons for all of us to think beyond ourselves. She teaches us to see the good in the world and to make the best of bad situations.

TO PERSUADE: Uruguay's president, José Mujica, should be the model for all national leaders. He lives in humble conditions, refuses to accept special treatment and is committed to social justice.

Supporting information

Supporting information convinces listeners of the arguments or ideas put forward in the introduction.

A. Read these examples of supporting information. With a partner, discuss which one has the most impact based on sentence variety and the use of emotional words.

FACT: What do you think of small businesses? They're not just hiding in shopping malls. As evidence, reflect on a 2013 *Forbes Magazine* article that found that an astounding 52 percent were home-based.

EXAMPLE: Colonel James Anderson unlocked his personal library to working boys including Andrew Carnegie. Carnegie put his learning to use. After making his fortune, he funded the construction of 2509 public libraries around the world.

ANECDOTE: A principal confessed that he only hired teachers with passion and love: passion for the subject and love for their students. Nothing else mattered.

Conclusion

If your purpose is to inform, a summary might be enough, perhaps suggesting where listeners might find further information.

> For further information, you may want to look at ... If you want to learn more, then ...

If your purpose is to inspire, ask listeners to reflect on what the message means to them.

> I hope this can change your life the way it's changed mine. Following this example can help you to ...

If the purpose of the presentation is to persuade, then the conclusion should feature a call to action that asks listeners to do something.

> Now is the time to make a change ... Your next step is to ...

B. Choose the sentence that you think is more likely to appeal to listeners. Then, discuss your choices with a partner.

1 INTRODUCING YOURSELF AS SPEAKER:
a) I'm Maria Green, a student at Acadia College and a trainee pilot.
b) My name is Maria Green and I'm a student at Acadia College.

2 INTRODUCING THE PRESENTATION:
a) I'm talking about Amelia Earhart, the first female pilot to fly across the Atlantic Ocean.
b) Amelia Earhart was only thirty-two when her plane disappeared on a 1937 attempt to fly around the world, but she left behind a remarkable set of achievements.

3 SUPPORTING INFORMATION:
a) I heard about Earhart when I was young in a book about female heroes.
b) Earhart was the first woman to fly solo from Hawaii to California. It was brave, considering six planes and ten lives had been lost during a race on the same route.

4 CONCLUSION:
a) Amelia Earhart's life teaches us to be courageous and brave enough to try something different.
b) Most people don't know Amelia Earhart had an interesting life.

> **!**
> *Pronunciation:
> Besides varying
> sentence length, use
> pauses and changes
> in pitch and volume
> to engage listeners.*

Amelia Earhart (1897–1937), checking equipment on her airplane in 1937

WARM-UP ASSIGNMENT
Introduce a Famous Brain

Marie Curie (1867–1924)

Part of what we know about the brain comes from studying people who have used their brains to make spectacular achievements. In Academic Survival Skill, you learned how to prepare an introduction to a presentation. Practise that skill now by introducing someone who is famous for intelligence and/or creativity.

A. Choose a famous thinker. Here are a few examples: Marie Curie, Albert Einstein, Stephen Hawking, Grace Hopper, Ada Lovelace, Alan Turing. Ask your teacher about choosing others.

B. Write a short description of your famous thinker. In your description, answer these questions:

• What is the person's name and title or position?

• What is the person famous for? Use the simple past and the present perfect tenses and signal words when describing aspects of the person's accomplishments. Review Focus on Grammar on page 73.

• What has the person done that distinguishes him or her as an intelligent and/or creative person?

C. Write an outline of your presentation. Keep listeners' attention by making good vocabulary choices and by varying the length of your sentences (see Focus on Speaking, page 78).

D. When you present, do not read from your notes. Use eye contact and good body language to show your enthusiasm for your topic. Practise your presentation on your own and then with a partner.

E. Present to the class. Ask for feedback to help you improve your presentation skills.

VOCABULARY BUILD 3	

A. Below are words from the Academic Word List that you will find in Listening 3. Highlight the words you understand and then circle the words you use.

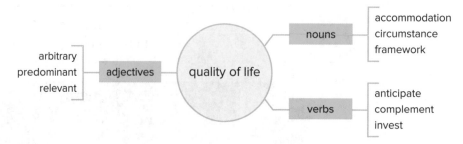

B. Draw an arrow (↓) to indicate where in each sentence the word in parentheses should be placed.

① (framework) A planning was used to organize the airport's construction.

② (relevant) Dr. Fowler considered the files before making her decision.

③ (predominant) Lack of workers was the reason the business failed to grow.

④ (circumstance) When a new arose, students had to reconsider their plan.

C. Choose the phrase that best completes each sentence. Key words are in bold.

1 One way to **invest** for the future is to _____.

a) enjoy your money while you can

b) save a little every month

c) borrow enough to live well

2 It was an **arbitrary** decision that was _____.

a) completely random

b) based on a clear plan

c) carefully thought through

3 To **complement** the staff already working there, the company _____.

a) told everyone how good they looked

b) dismissed half the staff

c) hired people with different skills

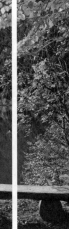

4 His **accommodation** in the country-side was a _____.

a) purple tent

b) new café

c) beautiful lake

5 One thing we could not **anticipate** was the _____.

a) rising of the sun

b) coming of winter

c) sudden snowstorm

My eLab ✎

Visit My eLab to complete Vocabulary Review exercises for this chapter.

LISTENING ③   **The Happy Ape**

In terms of happiness, most people think about different ways they could improve their lives. Some might think that certain possessions would make their lives easier or more interesting. Others might think that spending more time with friends or taking more vacation would be an improvement. Much research has been done to determine which factors improve quality of life and few have to do with spending money. In Listening 3, Dr. Sylvia Chen uses Robert Schalock's framework to explore the meaning of quality of life.

Before You Listen

A. Dr. Chen also points to an evolutionary basis for many of our behaviours. Write some ways in which our behaviours might be similar to those of the primates, like chimpanzees or apes. Then, discuss in a group.

_____

_____

_____

B. This excerpt from Listening 3 discusses emotional well-being. Why would university students be considered as "still shaping their personalities"?

> Let's begin with emotional well-being. It's a predominant factor for university students still shaping their personalities. Emotional well-being is tied up in self-concept—the mental pictures we carry about ourselves based on Sigmund Freud's ideas of the *id*, *ego* and *super-ego*. Let me briefly explain. *Id* is what you do by instinct, such as becoming angry. The *super-ego* considers what is right and moral. Your *ego* stands in the middle like a referee.

_____

_____

_____

C. These words and phrases will help you understand Listening 3. With a partner, discuss the meaning of each word or phrase and write its definition. Check your answers in a dictionary.

1 despair (n.): _____

_____

2 dictatorships (n.): _____

_____

3 inclusion (n.): _____

_____

4 mate (v.): _____

_____

5 moral compass (n.): _____

_____

_____

6 pursuit of happiness (n.): _____

_____

_____

7 safety of the treetops (n.): _____

_____

_____

8 teeter (v.): _____

_____

_____

While You Listen

D. The lecture describes eight factors that contribute to quality of life. The first time you listen, try to understand the general ideas. Listen a second time to take notes on each point in terms of how each relates to university students. Listen a third time to check your notes and add examples.

FRAMEWORK	NOTES
EMOTIONAL WELL-BEING	self-concept: *mental pictures of ourselves* _____ lack of stress: _____
INTERPERSONAL RELATIONS	relationships: _____ challenges: _____
MATERIAL WELL-BEING	possessions: _____ housing: _____
PERSONAL DEVELOPMENT	education: _____ performance: _____
PHYSICAL WELL-BEING	health and health care: _____ leisure: _____
SELF-DETERMINATION	autonomy/personal control and goals: _____ choices: _____
SOCIAL INCLUSION	community integration and participation: _____ _____
RIGHTS	legal rights, human rights, dignity, equality: _____ _____

After You Listen

E. In the lecture, Dr. Chen makes several references to primates, such as apes and chimpanzees. Answer the following questions. Then, discuss with a partner.

  1 In discussing *id, ego* and *super-ego*, Chen suggests our *super-ego* controls our anger. How does she relate this to primates?

      _____

      _____

  2 What is Chen's point in mentioning strength in numbers?

      _____

      _____

3 In terms of planning, how are people different from apes?

_____

_____

4 What does Chen mean when she says we might not have left the treetops had it not been for chemical rewards?

_____

_____

5 What does Chen suggest is a genetic difference in some people?

_____

_____

6 Why is the human ability to belong to several groups important?

_____

_____

7 Why is a fear of chaos important in both ape and human societies?

_____

_____

F. At the end of the lecture, Chen talks about some students dropping out and makes a suggestion. What is her suggestion and what more can you do?

_____

_____

FINAL ASSIGNMENT
Give an Academic Presentation

Use what you learned in this chapter to give an academic presentation on one aspect of research on the brain.

A. Start with the famous thinker you profiled in the Warm-Up Assignment. Based on the feedback you received from your teacher and classmates, consider how you can improve on the content and make revisions.

B. Build on your introduction by relating your famous thinker's accomplishments to an aspect of research you heard in one of this chapter's listenings. For example, if your famous thinker achieved greatness by thinking differently, refer to your notes to relate it to what Cadsby and others had to say about the brain. Decide what the purpose of your presentation will be: to inform, to inspire or to persuade. Refer to Academic Survival Skill on page 80.

C. Write an outline of your presentation. Add supporting information and a conclusion. Make good vocabulary choices and vary the length of your sentences (see Focus on Speaking, page 78). Use the simple past or the present perfect tense and signal words when describing how the person's accomplishments relate to one of the listenings. Review Focus on Grammar on page 73.

D. Practise your presentation with your notes and without them until you are confident. Then, practise with a partner.

E. Present to the class. Ask for feedback from your teacher and classmates.

How confident are you?

Think about what you learned in this chapter. Use the table to decide what you should review.

I LEARNED ...	I AM CONFIDENT	I NEED TO REVIEW
vocabulary related to mental and emotional health;	☐	☐
how to keep a listener's attention;	☐	☐
the simple past and present perfect tenses;	☐	☐
to infer meaning from context;	☐	☐
how to prepare and give an academic presentation.	☐	☐

VOCABULARY
Challenge

Think about the vocabulary and ideas in this chapter. Use these words to write two sentences about building a better brain.

altering	appreciate	categorize	complement	integrated	relevant

_____

_____

_____

_____

_____

_____

My eLab

Visit My eLab to build on what you learned.

CHAPTER 5
Inventing the Future

What's the next big thing? Once in a while, a new technology completely changes the world. In their day, steam engines and electric lights had this kind of impact, as did televisions, mobile phones and the Internet. It's sometimes hard to spot an influential technology at first because it can have a long incubation —the time it takes to go from an idea to widespread practical use. But 3D printing seems to be a technology that is likely to grow bigger as applications to many different fields are explored.

How will your future be printed?

In this chapter, you will

- learn vocabulary related to 3D printing;
- use register and tone to communicate effectively;
- listen to build schema;
- practise different sentence types;
- develop teamwork skills;
- give a presentation;
- plan and take part in meetings.

GEARING UP

A. Look at the image and then answer the questions.

A 3D printer makes sections of a model of the Eiffel Tower

1 3D printing is popular for making decorative items. What are some of its more serious applications?

_____

_____

2 Why might copyright be a concern with consumer use of 3D printers?

_____

_____

3 3D printing can work with a variety of materials, including sugar and chocolate. What advantages would there be in being able to print a dessert?

_____

_____

4 Why would 3D printers be important in places such as an aircraft carrier or a space station?

_____

_____

B. Discuss the questions and your answers, first with a partner, then in a group.

Using Register and Tone

A common expression about communicating is, "It's not what you say; it's how you say it." Register and tone refer to how you express yourself and both are ways through which you share your ideas more effectively.

Register

There are three forms of register: formal, informal and neutral. Choose register based on your purpose for speaking and who you are speaking with.

Use *formal register* with strangers and if you need to appear more serious when speaking to authority figures, such as a boss. Formal register avoids contractions (e.g., *I've*, *couldn't*) and slang (e.g., *cool*, *awesome*) and uses longer sentences. Formal register focuses on saying words fully and correctly, using proper grammar.

> We insist that medical professionals embrace three-dimensional printing in order to tailor implants such as articulated knees.

Use *informal register* in casual situations, in everyday conversations and with friends and others you know well. It's more common to use slang and informal contractions such as "gonna," "wanna" or "watcha doin'?" instead of "going to," "want to" or "what are you doing?" Grammar is less important, as long as you are properly understood. Shorter sentences are common when using informal register.

> The coolest thing about 3D printing is your doctor will someday make you the perfect fit of an artificial knee and other goodies.

Use *neutral register* when you explain facts, such as scientific processes. For this reason, neutral register avoids opinions. Neutral register is similar to formal register in avoiding contractions and slang. Jargon (professional terminology) is common in all three registers, but should only be used if you know your audience will understand it. For example, doctors can be more precise and save time with each other by using specific medical jargon rather than more commonly understood forms (e.g., *myocardial infarction* instead of *heart attack*).

> The term three-dimensional (3D) printing refers to a process that can be used to create objects such as artificial body parts which can be tailored for each individual.

A. Indicate whether these statements are formal, informal or neutral.

STATEMENTS	FORMAL	INFORMAL	NEUTRAL
❶ We're just hanging out at the lab today.	☐	☐	☐
❷ An MRI scan of a patient involves three steps.	☐	☐	☐
❸ The key role of the scientist is to ask questions.	☐	☐	☐
❹ 3D printing is never going to replace hand-carving.	☐	☐	☐
❺ After one hour, a prototype emerges from the printer.	☐	☐	☐
❻ Innovation is a principle driver in manufacturing.	☐	☐	☐

Tone

Tone refers to choosing words that express emotion (e.g., *anger, excitement, sorrow*) or degrees of professionalism (e.g., *confidence, intelligence, expertise*). Add tone by using words that carry greater weight in a speech or conversation.

B. Highlight the word or phrase in parentheses that best expresses the emotion or professionalism of the key words in bold. Look up words you don't know in a dictionary. Then, practise saying the sentences with a partner.

1 **concern:** We were (anxious / worried) when we couldn't find our pet snake.

2 **defiance:** They (don't want / absolutely refuse) to enter the last cave.

3 **fear:** I am (afraid / terrified) that he will make a mistake while skydiving.

4 **happiness:** At first, the young couple seemed (jubilant / happy) together.

5 **interest:** The scientist was (obsessed with / curious about) the new ant species.

6 **regret:** The librarian was (sorry / miserable) at the sight of the burnt books.

VOCABULARY BUILD 1

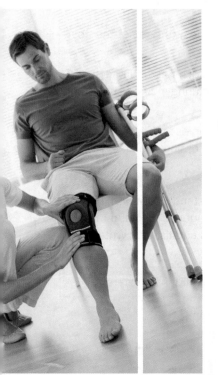

A. Below are words and phrases from the Academic Word List that you will find in Listening 1. Highlight the words you understand and then circle the words you use.

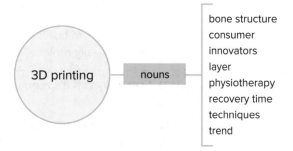

3D printing — nouns

- bone structure
- consumer
- innovators
- layer
- physiotherapy
- recovery time
- techniques
- trend

B. Fill in the blanks with the correct word or phrase to complete the paragraph. Use a dictionary for words you don't understand.

bone structure	physiotherapy	recovery time	trend

One of the problems with replacement parts for knees and other joints is that everyone has a different _____. Sometimes the artificial knee is too large or too small and needs to be replaced. This can lead to a longer _____ for a patient. During this time, long sessions of _____ are used to help the patient regain strength. But a new _____ is to create custom knees using 3D printers that reduce care after an operation.

C. Choose the word or phrase that best completes each sentence. Key words are in bold.

1 As a **consumer**, I want to make sure that I (offer / get) the best deal when I shop.

2 True **innovators** (build on / copy) what others have done.

3 By depositing plastic drops one **layer** at a time, a (negative / positive) shape is formed.

4 3D printing involves **techniques** developed to create things (randomly / consistently).

3D Printing

On April 3, 1973, Martin Cooper (1928–) made a mobile phone call—the first ever. Ten years later, Cooper and his team introduced mobile phones to the general public. He could not have predicted the countless features inventors would add, such as cameras, music players and social media apps. Similarly, 3D printing is an invention that many people are now developing in surprising ways. Listening 1 discusses some of the 3D printing applications, from engine bolts to artificial knees.

Before You Listen

A. A *prototype* is a preliminary model that helps designers figure out problems before constructing a finished model for mass production. Look around you and imagine how 3D printing could be used to make a prototype for common objects such as pen, a watch, a pair of glasses or a mobile phone. How might that prototype improve the design? Discuss in a group.

B. Read this excerpt from Listening 1. What types of jobs that people do now might 3D printing eventually replace? Discuss your answer with a partner.

> **NIGEL SOUTHWAY:** If it's a good technology, it's supposed to make the cost go down.
>
> **MAKDA GHEBRESLASSIE:** Nigel Southway is with the society of manufacturing engineers. He says 3D printing will make the manufacturing industry more efficient, but there is a price to pay.
>
> **NS:** Some of the artisan techniques of toolmaking examples may disappear, and some of the complexity of running certain kinds of processing equipment won't be necessary with this technology; it's more hands-off.

C. Knowing these words and phrases will help you understand Listening 1. For example, *magnetic resonance imaging* (MRI) uses a magnetic field and radio waves to create detailed images of your body's organs and tissues. Write each word under its image.

bolts	crutches	engine block	MRI	scars

_____ _____ _____ _____ _____

While You Listen

D. The first time you listen, write the initials of the person speaking and take notes on what each speaker is saying. Use this table to replace names with initials. Listen a second time and indicate whether each speaker uses formal, informal or neutral register. Listen a third time to review your notes and add details.

INITIALS	NAME	FORMAL	INFORMAL	NEUTRAL
LG	Linda Gagnier	☐	☐	☐
MG	Makda Ghebreslassie	☐	☐	☐
NS	Nigel Southway	☐	☐	☐
JT	John Tenbusch	☐	☐	☐
JU	Jill Urbanic	☐	☐	☐

SPEAKER	NOTES
MG	technical issues with cellphone holders
	hip, knees replaced
	technology changing
	knee implant
	prototype made using a 3D metal printer
	machine lays down a layer of thin, powdered metal
	use 3D printer to make food, design art
	MRI of your good knee
	industrial ones expensive; consumer ones, too
	students designing an engine block
	loss of some jobs
	create customized 3D objects
	files shared wrong hands
	it's not the tool itself
	as 3D technology evolves

After You Listen

E. Choose the phrase that best completes each sentence.

① CBC's Makda Ghebreslassie suggests 3D printing has _____ applications.

    a) educational, military and entertainment

    b) aerospace, industrial and personal

    c) aerospace, military and medical

② The trouble with traditional knee replacements is they _____.

    a) are likely to break down as the plastic is weak

    b) are either too large or too small for most patients

    c) can be rejected by the body and need to be replaced

③ Unlike a plastic printer that drops heated plastic, a metal printer _____.

    a) uses a laser to weld together powdered metal

    b) uses a laser to cut away a solid metal block

    c) forms a shape by dripping melted metal

④ Astronauts are most likely to use a 3D printer _____.

    a) to create food to eat, such as pizza

    b) to create tools to do new experiments

    c) to replace parts that are damaged

⑤ When students create their own metal bolts, they can make them _____.

    a) for about the same price

    b) for much less money

    c) at a higher cost

⑥ Although it's likely some jobs will be lost because of 3D printing, _____.

    a) those who own 3D printers are less likely to need work

    b) 3D printers will be used in education to teach new skills

    c) other jobs will be created in design and engineering

⑦ The example of the 3D printed gun _____.

    a) shows why sales of 3D printers should be tightly controlled

    b) explains that a new technology can have good and bad uses

    c) suggests that traditional guns and weapons will disappear

F. Read the following statements and choose the best summary of Listening 1.

☐ The future of 3D printers is most likely to be in large industrial models that can be used to work with metal and other materials.

☐ As a tool, the 3D printer is likely to change many fields as inventors think of new ways to use it.

☐ The home 3D printer is likely to disappear as commercial models become more convenient for everyone.

FOCUS ON GRAMMAR

Sentence Types

As you heard in Listening 1, speakers used a mixture of simple, compound, complex and compound-complex sentences. The purpose was to give variety to what they had to say and to maintain their listeners' attention. However, when listening to speakers, it can be difficult to unravel complex and compound-complex sentences. It helps to listen for the conjunctions, those parts of speech that connect clauses.

There are two kinds of clauses: independent and dependent. An *independent clause* has a subject and a verb and expresses a complete thought. A *dependent clause* can have both a subject and a verb, but it does not express a complete thought.

> **!**
>
> *Use the acronym "fanboys" to remember the coordinate conjunctions: for, and, nor, but, or, yet, so.*

SENTENCE TYPE	STRUCTURE	EXAMPLE
SIMPLE	one independent clause	3D printing is now available on campus.
COMPOUND	two independent clauses linked by a coordinate conjunction (*for, and, nor, but, or, yet, so*)	3D printing is now available **but** it's not being used by many students.
COMPLEX	independent clause plus a dependent clause, linked by a subordinate conjunction (*for example, as, after, although, because, instead of, since, when, until*)	3D printing is now available **since** the Engineering Association contributed two thousand dollars.
COMPOUND-COMPLEX	two (or more) independent clauses linked by a coordinate conjunction and at least one dependent clause linked by a subordinate conjunction	3D printing is now available **but** using it can be expensive **because** of the cost of materials.

A. Imagine you are listening to someone say the following compound, complex and compound-complex sentences. Highlight the conjunctions and underline the clauses. Then, write the sentence type.

SENTENCE TYPE

1 As new technologies become more popular, they also tend to become less expensive. _____

2 Odd as it sounds, cooking seems complex, but it is staggeringly simple. _____

3 Matt Griffin says it's not as hard as it looks and that the technology has been around a lot longer than we think. _____

4 Layer after layer of plastic is built up until it assumes the shape of, say, a hubcap. _____

5 As patents expired, it became feasible to spin off a number of cheap consumer-grade 3D printers. _____

B. Read the following sets of sentences and use conjunctions to combine each set into a compound or a complex sentence.

Pronunciation: MIT (Massachusetts Institute of Technology) is an initialism; you pronounce its letters. NASA (National Aeronautics and Space Administration) is an acronym; you pronounce it as a word.

1. 3D printing technology evolved. People started to think about more than just designing cars.

   COMPLEX: _____

   _____

2. He's a professor at MIT. He remembers why people first started thinking about it.

   COMPOUND: _____

   _____

3. I came to MIT in 1986. Manufacturing was moving overseas.

   COMPLEX: _____

   _____

4. The RepRap project started. They wanted a 3D printer that could print out parts to build another 3D printer.

   COMPOUND: _____

   _____

Use what you learned about sentence types when you prepare assignments.

5. Ordinary people got their hands on ever-cheaper printers. The new technology began to change the way people made things.

   COMPLEX: _____

   _____

VOCABULARY BUILD 2

A. Below are words from the Academic Word List that you will find in Listening 2. Highlight the words you understand and then circle the words you use.

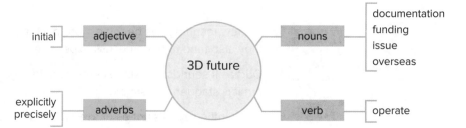

initial — adjective

3D future

nouns — documentation, funding, issue, overseas

explicitly, precisely — adverbs

verb — operate

B. Highlight the word or phrase in parentheses that best completes each sentence. Key words are in bold.

1. Reliability (is / is not) an **issue** when you need something to work for years.

2. Jobs were moving **overseas** because costs were (higher / lower) there.

3. She had an **initial** idea that was used instead of a/an (later / earlier) one.

4. The problem with the 3D printer was solved by (reviewing / writing) the **documentation**.

C. Fill in the blanks with the words that have the closest meaning to the phrases in bold.

explicitly	funding	precisely	operate

1 We approached the government to obtain **a donation of money to support**

(_____) the project.

2 The instructions to the contestants were given **in great and clear detail**

(_____).

3 They were all worried about how long the engine would **continue to function**

(_____).

4 She chose her words of goodbye **with great care and attention**

(_____).

D. VOCABULARY EXTENSION: *Overseas* is an example of a compound word—a word made up of two or more smaller words. Write a definition for each compound word and then use a vertical line to separate it.

1 air │ craft: _____

2 backdrop: _____

3 desktop: _____

4 hubcap: _____

5 inkjet: _____

6 software: _____

The Revolution Will Be Extruded

As new technologies become popular, they often become less expensive. This is due, in part, to more competition as patents (legal rights to the ideas behind a new technology) expire, making the techniques and plans freely available to everyone. As inventors look at old patents, they find ways to improve and create newer innovative products. Users of 3D printers also drive innovation as they come up with new applications for the technology. Listening 2 explores the history of 3D printing and talks about new applications.

Before You Listen

A. The title of Listening 2 uses the words *revolution* and *extruded*. A *revolution* is a dramatic and wide-ranging change. To *extrude* something is to push material through a shaped opening to form a 3D object; it's one technique in 3D printing. What changes might 3D printing make in your life in the next five years? Discuss your answer with a partner.

B. Read the opening comments of Listening 2 and highlight the applications of 3D printing that Cory Doctorow talks about. Discuss those that are unfamiliar with your partner.

CORY DOCTOROW: The metaphor of 3D printing, which is to say that you have a machine, and you load it up with some kind of stock, and the machine places the stock very precisely and does something to join it up with the bits that it's just placed down, has branched out into medicine where you have people, not just 3D printing titanium prostheses, like jaw bones for people who've had part of their skulls removed due to cancer, or other injuries or insults, but all the way up to placing human tissue on a lattice where it can grow in order to produce artificial organs. You have it in food where there's this idea of taking powdered feed stocks and then placing them very precisely and assembling them into things like pizzas and so on. There's this person who claims he's going to make a 3D printer for pizza in answer to a NASA challenge.

C. These words will help you understand Listening 2. Match each word to its definition.

WORDS		DEFINITIONS
1 geeks	_____	a) legal rights to the ideas behind a new technology
2 intend	_____	b) exactly as said
3 literally	_____	c) advanced
4 patents	_____	d) plan to do something
5 savvy	_____	e) condition or requirement
6 sophisticated	_____	f) term for those obsessed with technology
7 stipulation	_____	g) having expert practical knowledge about something

While You Listen

D. Before you listen, read the headings in the notes column of the table to see what you will be expected to write. These headings include comparisons and explanations for key phrases as well as consequences and definitions. The first time you listen, take notes. Listen a second time and indicate the register of each speaker. Listen a third time to review your notes and add details.

SPEAKER	FORMAL	INFORMAL	NEUTRAL
Cory Doctorow	☐	☐	☐
Narrator	☐	☐	☐
Person	☐	☐	☐
Matt Griffin	☐	☐	☐
Michael Sima	☐	☐	☐

MIT (Massachusetts Institute of Technology)

KEY PHRASES	NOTES
Ink-jet printers spread out a thin layer of ink to make words and pictures.	COMPARISON: *3D printing adds layers of plastic to make a shape.*
Little spaghetti strands of plastic ...	COMPARISON:
3D machines aren't sophisticated, but ...	EXPLANATION:
You don't need to be a coder.	EXPLANATION:
A thirty-year history of 3D printing ...	EXPLANATION:
When patents expired ...	CONSEQUENCE:
MIT professor Michael Sima worked on 3D printing technologies thirty years ago.	CONSEQUENCE:
In 1986, manufacturing and product design were moving overseas.	CONSEQUENCE:
In the late 1980s, Japanese were designing new cars twice as fast as Americans (Nagoya vs. Detroit).	CONSEQUENCE:
3D printing technology evolved ...	CONSEQUENCE:
3D printing potential for where it might be hard to buy or carry things ...	EXAMPLE:
A printer plus raw materials and you could make your own replacement parts ...	CONSEQUENCE:
Early models had problems but were still impressive ...	EXPLANATION:
Biggest early issue was reliability ...	QUESTION: *How long would it operate before something needed to be repaired?*
Making these things layer by layer, reliability is very important.	EXPLANATION:

KEY PHRASES	NOTES
British printing geeks came up with the RepRap (replicating rapid prototype) ...	CONSEQUENCE:
The RepRap idea ...	PURPOSE:
Open source hardware ...	DEFINITION:
Patents expired.	CONSEQUENCE:
People got cheaper printers.	CONSEQUENCE:

After You Listen

E. Indicate whether these statements are true or false, according to the listening.

STATEMENTS	TRUE	FALSE
1 Ink-jet printers and 3D printers work on the same principle.	☐	☐
2 Inexpensive 3D printers are as good as expensive ones.	☐	☐
3 Most people assume 3D printing was invented a long time ago.	☐	☐
4 People were impressed by the products made by early 3D printers.	☐	☐
5 If a 3D printer breaks down, you can fix it and keep printing the same job.	☐	☐
6 The RepRap idea was to have a 3D printer that could make its own replacement parts.	☐	☐
7 MakerBot became available after early patents expired.	☐	☐
8 Unfortunately, cheaper printers have made printing more complicated.	☐	☐

F. Number these statements in chronological order (in order of time).

_____ British geeks built on MIT experience to create RepRap.

_____ Competition created interest in 3D printing.

_____ Patents expired, opening opportunities for cheaper printers.

___*1*___ American manufacturing and design jobs started moving overseas.

_____ Early printers had problems, but were still impressive.

_____ Japanese designed cars in half the time it took American designers.

Developing Teamwork Skills

One important skill to develop is the ability to work successfully in groups. Group participants consider themselves and others as team members. Each member may have one or more jobs to do, but together the group shares the common goal of completing a task. That task might include thinking of a new idea, solving a problem, answering a question or making a proposal. Teamwork can help develop leadership and problem-solving skills, and encourage co-operation and conflict resolution.

A. Read these techniques for how to work successfully as a team. Then, answer the questions that follow. Discuss your answers with a partner.

Agree on the task so that everyone has a common idea of what needs to be done. If you have been given an assignment, make sure team members are clear about the details, including short-term and final deadlines. An agenda can help (see an example in the Final Assignment, page 108).

Agree on roles for each team member. For example, one might take the role of the chair (meeting leader), one the role of the recorder/secretary (taking notes on what is discussed and agreed).

Listen actively to understand what a team member is saying. As with schema building (see Focus on Listening, page 103), compare what is being said to what you already know and decide if the information is new and whether or not it contradicts what you previously thought.

Ask questions in formal or neutral register. Informal register can lead to misunderstandings. The tone of your questions and comments should be respectful. Use group meetings to learn from other team members.

Support other members when they make a good point or suggestion. Offer words of encouragement. Share ideas that support team effort.

Manage conflict by analyzing root causes. Conflicts sometimes happen because one team member doesn't understand or like the tasks, the roles or the decisions of the team. In other cases, one team member may have had problems with another team member. Rather than ignore problems, it's best to confront them and find a solution so the work can proceed.

1 What might go wrong if some team members don't understand the assignment?

_____

_____

2 *Devil's advocate*, *timekeeper* and *jargon buster* are three other roles. Write definitions for each. Then, list three other roles team members might play at a meeting.

_____

_____

_____

_____

_____

3 What can be done if team members refuse to accept the group's ideas, perhaps preferring one of their own?

_____

_____

4 What should be done if one team member uses a lot of jargon that others in the group do not understand?

_____

_____

5 When team members deserve recognition, how does it help everyone to praise them?

_____

_____

B. In a group, read the three conflicts and discuss how you would handle each one.

CONFLICT 1: One team member refuses to accept the group's understanding of the task and its details.

CONFLICT 2: One team member avoids responsibilities: does not fully participate and misses deadlines.

CONFLICT 3: One team member is unhappy with a particular role and is disruptive and is delaying the project.

WARM-UP ASSIGNMENT
Develop Product Proposals

In this Warm-Up Assignment, form groups of three and design a product suitable for 3D printing using metal, plastic or wood. The product you design should help people living in shelters after a disaster, such as an earthquake, a flood or a tsunami.

A. In your group, brainstorm for ideas; encourage suggestions for different options without criticizing. Use the teamwork skills you learned in Academic Survival Skill. Remember to use a variety of sentence types (see Focus on Grammar, page 95) to make your ideas more engaging.

B. Together, decide on the three best 3D printing job ideas (one each for metal, plastic and wood) and have each group member choose one to present in the Final Assignment meeting (page 107).

C. Prepare notes on the products to be printed. Use this format.

My choice of 3D printed product is _____. This product would be printed in (metal, plastic, wood). I believe it would help people living in shelters after a/an (earthquake, flood or tsunami) because ...

> _During a natural disaster, many people will lose their eyeglasses. These could be 3D printed in plastic._

D. Practise your presentation with your group. Use formal register and respectful tone as you learned in Focus on Speaking (page 90).

E. Ask for feedback from your group members on how you could improve your presentation. As a group, reflect on how successful you were in working as a team.

Building Schema

Schema theory is based on the idea that when you learn something, you connect it to other things you know. A schema is a series of related ideas and experiences. For example, when you hear the word *technology*, words and pictures appear in your mind.

A. Look at the schema map (also called a mind map) on technology and add circles with related ideas. Then, share your ideas with a partner.

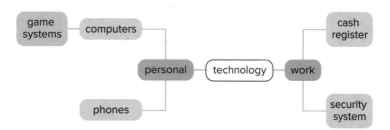

In your schema, you probably came up with different ideas than your partner. This is because you each made different connections to prior knowledge and experience.

Here are tips to improve your understanding when you listen.

- Before you listen to any presentation, think about what you know about the speaker and the topic. If you have the title of a presentation, consider how it relates to your experience.

- While you listen, think about what the ideas in the presentation mean to you: how they are important to similar ideas and how they are important in a wider context, such as to others around the world.

- While you listen, take notes on a schema map. Everything you hear is either something you know, something you don't know or something you thought you knew but might be wrong about. Be open to ideas that are new or different. Add these to your schema map. Think of questions, examples and evidence that would help you build on prior knowledge.

> *After taking notes on a schema, rewrite them, adding details.*

B. Read this excerpt from Listening 3 and answer the questions that follow, keeping the tips above in mind. Then, compare answers in a group.

> In a June, 2014 article, journalist Kwame Opam discussed the Nestlé Corporation's plans to, and I quote Opam directly here, "to develop a device that scans people's individual levels of nutrients and designs food around their needs, not unlike the replicators found on Starfleet spaceships."

1. What do you think about when you hear or see the word *journalist*?

_____

_____

2. Do you know anything about the Nestlé Corporation? Can you think of any products that it produces?

_____

_____

3. What do you imagine when you see the word *device* in this context?

_____

_____

4. Have you heard of replicators and Starfleet spaceships? Whether you have or have not, what do you think of when you imagine them?

_____

_____

VOCABULARY BUILD 3

A. Below are words from the Academic Word List that you will find in Listening 3. Highlight the words you understand and then circle the words you use.

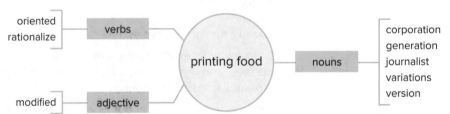

oriented / rationalize → **verbs**

modified → **adjective**

→ printing food →

nouns → corporation / generation / journalist / variations / version

B. Choose the synonym (word with a similar meaning) for the word in bold in each sentence.

1. There are many **variations** among 3D printers based on the materials they print.

   a) similarities   b) differences   c) opportunities

2. The **corporation** had a responsibility to its shareholders to develop new products.

   a) business   b) inventor   c) employees

3. The **journalist** refused to give up the name of her source.

   a) editor   b) reporter   c) correspondent

4. We were able to **rationalize** the cost of the 3D printer because we could rent it out.

   a) justify   b) diminish   c) increase

C. Highlight the best definition for each word. Use a dictionary to check your answers.

1 version
a) older form of something
b) particular form of something

2 modified
a) traditionally and naturally grown
b) changed from its original natural form

3 generation
a) people born at the same time
b) continuously recreate something

4 oriented
a) set in the direction of something
b) set in the direction of Asia

Visit My eLab to complete Vocabulary Review exercises for this chapter.

LISTENING 3 Printing the Edible

Herman Potočnik (1892–1929) was an early rocket scientist who imagined a series of orbiting satellites that could be used to bounce radio signals around the world. It took thirty years for his dream to become a reality; today, it's a critical part of our ability to communicate, watch television and use the Internet. The world needs dreamers to imagine the future as well as others who can build it. In Listening 3, learn how 3D printing was also imagined by science fiction writers, years before it became a reality.

Before You Listen

A. On a separate page, draw a schema map on 3D printing (see Focus on Listening, task A, page 103, for a model). Use the schema map to note what you already know about 3D printing as well as what you are unsure of or don't know. You can use different colours to explore these ideas. After you listen, add to your schema map.

B. 3D printers have been compared to *replicators*, science fiction machines that can make almost anything, including a wide range of foods. Read this excerpt from Listening 3 and discuss in a group whether or not you would want a food replicator at home.

> Artificial meats. Labs are growing and testing them now. But similar ideas have been around for centuries. Some Chinese vegetarian restaurants offer all varieties of meat and fish made from soybeans, mushrooms and other non-meat ingredients; the look, the taste and the flavours are nearly identical.

C. These words and phrases will help you understand Listening 3. Read each word and phrase and its definition. Then, use each in a sentence.

1 nutrients (n.): substances that are necessary for growth

Proteins, carbohydrates, fats and vitamins are all essential nutrients.

2 revived (v.): brought back to life

_____

_____

3 planetary colonists (n.): travellers who will start civilization on another planet

_____

_____

4 counterpart (n.): something (or someone) with the same function

_____

_____

5 train of thought (n.): a series of related ideas

_____

_____

While You Listen

D. Use the timeline to summarize the ideas or innovations of the authors mentioned. Read the dates of their works first so you are ready when you hear them.

DATE	SOURCE	INNOVATION
1867	Jules Verne, *From the Earth to the Moon*	
1879	Edward Page Mitchell, *The Senator's Daughter*	
1912	Edgar Rice Burroughs, *A Princess of Mars*	
1913	L. Frank Baum, *The Patchwork Girl of Oz*	
1948	Robert Heinlein, *Space Cadet*	
1966–1969	Gene Roddenberry's television series *Star Trek*	
1995	Neil Stephenson, *The Diamond Age: Or a Young Lady's Illustrated Primer*	
2003	Margaret Atwood, *Oryx and Crake*	
2014	Kwame Opam, article	*Nestlé device scans people's nutrients and …*

After You Listen

E. Highlight the word or phrase in parentheses that best completes each sentence.

The earliest science fiction stories to talk about food mentioned (replicators / preserved foods). In one story, food was delivered by (robots / aliens). In other science fiction stories, food pills were used to provide many (tastes / meals) at once. Science fiction tended to follow scientific discoveries. For example, after microwave ovens were invented, they appeared in science fiction (one year / five years) later. Novels also tended to recognize social issues: the poor were fed by machines that used (seaweed / fish paste) as the main ingredient. But just as science fiction has sometimes followed science, the opposite is happening and a company called SMRC is developing a microwave oven-like device to feed (space travellers and colonists / sailors and polar explorers).

F. Number the following sentences in the correct order to create a summary of Listening 3.

_____ Babbage discusses the use of fish paste and genetically modified chickens.

___*1*___ Charles Preston interviews science fiction historian Sarah Babbage.

_____ Preston asks about early science fiction ideas on food in space.

_____ Babbage says she is not interested in having a machine to make her food.

_____ Preston asks Babbage about Starfleet.

_____ Babbage explains about preserved food, pills, robot waiters and microwave ovens.

_____ Babbage explains it's a reference to a TV series and a replicator.

FINAL ASSIGNMENT
Conduct a Meeting to Discuss Proposals

Meet with another group and present the 3D printed product proposals that your group developed in the Warm-Up Assignment.

A. Re-form your Warm-Up Assignment groups.

B. Join a second group and plan the meeting. Use Academic Survival Skill (page 101) techniques to work successfully as a team. Make sure everyone understands the purpose of the meeting and assign key roles.

C. As one group, decide on the meeting's agenda. Ask the recorder/secretary to take notes. Use this table as a model.

AGENDA	
TITLE OF THE MEETING	Choose the best 3D printed product proposal.
PLACE	
DATE/TIME	
BUSINESS (WHAT WILL BE DISCUSSED)	Each group member will present a proposal for a 3D printed product.
ROLES	Chair: _____ Recorder/Secretary: _____ Timekeeper: _____ Other: _____
PRESENTATIONS	PROPOSAL 1: _____ PROPOSAL 2: _____ PROPOSAL 3: _____ PROPOSAL 4: _____ PROPOSAL 5: _____ PROPOSAL 6: _____
GROUP DISCUSSION	Discuss the six proposals. Ask questions to get additional information or for clarification.
VOTE	As a group, vote for the best proposal. Note: group members cannot vote for their own proposal.

D. Follow the agenda. Have group members present their proposals. Other group members can ask questions, but the meeting leader and the timekeeper will need to pay attention to the amount of time available.

E. During the presentations and discussions, as group members, use a variety of sentence types (see Focus on Grammar, page 95) to make your ideas, comments and suggestions more engaging. Use formal or neutral register and a respectful tone (Focus on Speaking, page 90) to keep the meeting business-like.

F. When presentations are finished, as a group, vote for the best proposal.

G. Reflect on your presentation and how well you contributed to the group. What could you improve?

How confident
are you?

Think about what you learned in this chapter. Use the table to decide what you should review.

I LEARNED ...	I AM CONFIDENT	I NEED TO REVIEW
vocabulary related to 3D printing;	☐	☐
how to use register and tone;	☐	☐
how to build schema;	☐	☐
about different sentence types;	☐	☐
teamwork skills;	☐	☐
how to give a presentation;	☐	☐
how to plan and take part in meetings.	☐	☐

VOCABULARY
Challenge

Think about the vocabulary and ideas in this chapter. Use these words to write two sentences that summarize the future of 3D printing.

consumer	issue	modified	operate	trend	version

_____

_____

_____

_____

_____

_____

My eLab
Visit My eLab to build on what you learned.

CHAPTER 6

Engineering the Future

People have always created tools to improve their lives. Tools help us engage in a greater variety of tasks. In recent years, particular attention has turned to creating tools to help those who are differently abled, for example more personalized wheelchairs. New tools now allow us to track and understand DNA, medical and other fitness details. There are even opportunities to enhance our abilities, in some cases by implanting technology directly into the body.

How would you use technology to improve your health and fitness?

In this chapter, you will

- learn vocabulary related to health and fitness;
- predict and infer while listening;
- review conditional sentences;
- learn how to paraphrase and summarize;
- summarize an interview;
- use aids when speaking;
- participate in a group discussion.

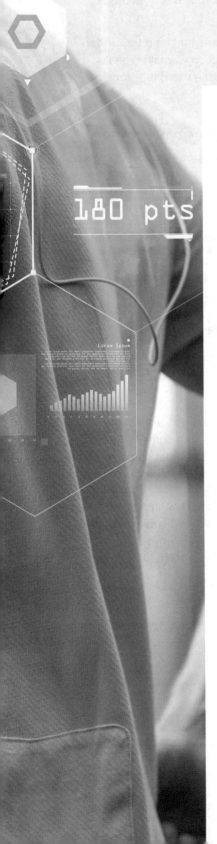

GEARING UP

A. Look at the illustration and then answer the questions.

Activity tracker data

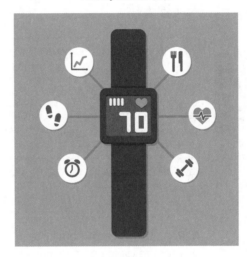

1 Why might you want to count your steps using an activity tracker?

_____

_____

2 The knife and fork indicate how much energy (calories) you are using. What other information do you need to make sense of this data?

_____

_____

3 The graph icon shows the amount of daily activity. How many minutes of activity do you estimate you do each day? _____

4 Many people are enthusiastic about activity trackers initially but then abandon them later. Why might this be?

_____

_____

B. Discuss the questions and your answers, first with a partner, then in a group.

Predicting and Inferring Ideas

The concepts *predicting* and *inferring* are about guessing. Before you listen, you predict what you will hear based on your knowledge of the speaker, the title of the topic and the context of the presentation. For example, you may know the speaker's level of expertise and you may have some ideas about the topic. The title may give you a clue about the speaker's point of view. The context, such as a classroom, a political meeting room or a club, may help you predict as well.

While you listen, you make inferences—informed guesses that help you understand the meaning of what is said. Much of this is based on what the speaker says and how it's said. Look at the following table. Practise using the signal words and phrases in sentences with a partner.

DOES THE SPEAKER	SIGNAL WORDS AND PHRASES AND OTHER INDICATORS
state opinions?	I think / I feel / Some people agree / It's widely thought / I have to say
state facts?	According to / It's well known that / Everyone knows / Research shows
explain the speech's purpose?	My reason for speaking today … / I'd like to explain … / A problem we face is [followed by a solution].
stress some words or phrases more than others?	Some people *might* think … / It was the *first* issue … / The *most* important point …
emphasize points with gestures or expressions?	pointing / slicing the air with one's hands / nodding or shaking one's head / smiling or frowning
avoid some topics?	We don't have time to talk about … / I'm not going to explain … / We don't have time to discuss … [or no mention of the topic].

A. Read this excerpt from Listening 2. Mark the point where you are able to infer the topic being discussed by the words and ideas that come before it. Then, from the above table, identify what the speaker says that helps you infer meaning.

> If I can just backtrack for a moment, let me explain how I became interested in this topic. I'd have to say that I blame my father. When I was young, my father—who wore thick glasses—jokingly called me his "eagle-eyed daughter." At the time, I wondered what it would be like to have an eagle's vision and, with a little research, I found out.

_____

_____

_____

_____

_____

_____

B. Read these statements from the listenings. Discuss with a partner what you might infer from each one.

- However, for you to accomplish [an eagle's] wide vision feat would mean repositioning your eyes on the sides of your head.
- I understand that we've made a lot of progress since then.
- It's believed that Leonardo da Vinci (1452–1519) was responsible for the idea for the first pedometer, a mechanical tool that measures steps.
- The newest models [of activity trackers] have sensors to detect motion in three dimensions, using what's called a *three-access accelerometer*; that's the biggest difference from the old-generation pedometers.

VOCABULARY BUILD 1

A. Below are words from the Academic Word List that you will find in Listening 1. Highlight the words you understand and then circle the words you use.

accurate
resolved — **adjectives**

intensely — **adverb**

tracking activity

nouns — access
achievements
dimensions

verbs — registering
underestimate

B. Match each word to its definition.

WORDS		DEFINITIONS
❶ achievements	_____	a) detecting something
❷ dimensions	_____	b) with extreme force or strength
❸ intensely	_____	c) things done successfully that make you proud
❹ registering	_____	d) aspects of something

C. Choose the phrase that best completes each sentence. Key words are in bold.

❶ The problem was **resolved** at the meeting, so _____.
   a) they continued to discuss it
   b) no more needed to be said
   c) it seemed unsolvable

❷ After repeating the experiment, the results were shown to be **accurate** and _____.
   a) were accepted by everyone
   b) made the scientists try again
   c) had to be thrown out

3 It was a mistake to **underestimate** her strength _____.

  a) as she was unable to lift 10 kilograms

  b) because everyone knew she was weak

  c) as she easily lifted 50 kilograms

4 In terms of **access** to the building, _____.

  a) everyone could use the front door

  b) there was no way to get in

  c) people could exit underground

LISTENING ❶   Activity Trackers and Apps

It's believed that Leonardo da Vinci (1452–1519) was responsible for the idea for the first pedometer, a mechanical tool that measures steps. The modern equivalent is the activity tracker, a device that builds on the mechanical pedometer to estimate everything from the calories you burn to your sleep patterns. By giving you feedback on your exercise routines, sleep habits and state of well-being, activity trackers aim to motivate you to lead a healthier life. In Listening 1, longevity columnist Sharon Basaraba reviews the best features of several activity trackers.

Before You Listen

A. Activity trackers typically measure heart rate, calories burned and distances covered, both in steps and kilometres. What would be the practical benefits of knowing such information?

_____

_____

_____

_____

_____

B. To *extrapolate* means to use one idea to understand a larger one. If one kilo of food was enough for three people, you could "extrapolate" to suggest that ten kilos would be enough for thirty people. A global positioning system (GPS) uses satellites to track one's location. Together with an accelerometer (a speed measuring device that tracks motion), an activity tracker can tell how far and how fast you go. Read this excerpt from Listening 1 and then number the activities in order of the effort required (1 = most effort; 4 = least effort).

> Those old ones [pedometers] used an internal ball mechanism that you would hear click; it would activate a switch every time you took a step. Those were essentially just step counters, so any data on distance and calories burned were just extrapolated out of the number of steps you took. The new ones use this accelerometer technology along with GPS positioning, to figure out how much movement you're doing of any kind—are you standing, sitting, lying down, fidgeting?—along with how intensely you're exerting yourself.

_____ sitting   _____ sleeping   _____ standing   _____ walking

C. These words and phrases will help you understand Listening 1. Read the definitions and then use each word or phrase in a sentence. Discuss your sentences with a partner.

WORDS/PHRASES	DEFINITIONS	SENTENCES
1 caveats (n.)	warnings about rules or limits	
2 cumbersome (adj.)	too large or heavy to be useful	
3 discrepancy (n.)	lack of agreement between facts	
4 ICU (n.)	intensive care unit (in a hospital)	
5 longevity (n.)	long life	
6 notoriously (adv.)	widely and unfavourably; infamously	
7 obtrusive (adj.)	standing out in an unwelcome way	
8 sleep apnea (n.)	temporary pause in breathing when sleeping	
9 thermogenesis (n.)	production of heat by a human or animal body	

While You Listen

D. Listening 1 is about the different features of activity trackers. Before you listen, read the topics and predict what you think each will be about. Write brief predictions in the first column. The first time you listen to the interview, try to understand the gist. Listen a second time and take notes. Listen a third time to see what you can infer from your notes in terms of informed guesses. You will use your notes to write a summary in the Warm-Up Assignment.

TOPICS	NOTES
BEYOND PEDOMETERS	safety strap
ACTIVITY TRACKER DIFFERENCES	NEAT: non-exercise activity thermogenesis overestimates activity by _____

TOPICS	NOTES
SMARTPHONES	drawbacks:
SLEEP QUALITY	won't diagnose _____ restless doesn't = _____
ACCURACY	Harvard researcher: _____
EVIDENCE	2007 study: _____

After You Listen

E. Answer these questions. Then, discuss with a partner.

1 Why does the interviewer think people might consider an electronic activity monitor?

_____

_____

2 Besides pedometers that clip to your waistband, what other ways does Basaraba say you can wear activity trackers?

_____

_____

3 What are some companies doing to make activity trackers more attractive?

_____

_____

4 What is a special advantage of the disposable activity tracker?

_____

_____

5 To what kinds of activity does non-exercise activity thermogenesis refer?

_____

_____

6 What is the main attraction of using a phone over an activity tracker?

_____

_____

7 What do sleep apps measure in terms of activity?

_____

_____

8 Why does Basaraba mention that the activity trackers do not detect sleep apnea? Make an inference.

_____

_____

Develop Your Vocabulary: When you are trying to learn a new word, use it ten or more times in your conversations and writing to help remember it.

F. Based on everything you have heard and read, work in a group to design the perfect activity tracker that includes all the features mentioned in Listening 1. Think of other features that would make it better.

FOCUS ON GRAMMAR

Conditional Sentences

Conditional sentences are used to imagine what could happen, what might have happened, and what you wish would happen. Conditional sentences generally have two parts: an *if*-clause and a result clause. This sentence, paraphrased from Listening 1, is an example of a conditional sentence:

> If you've resolved to sit less and stand more, you might consider an activity monitor.

There are three conditional forms. Read the explanations and examples to understand when and how to use them.

CONDITIONAL FORMS	USED	*IF*-CLAUSE VERB TENSE	RESULT CLAUSE VERB TENSE
FIRST CONDITIONAL	for general truths and automatic results	simple present If I **exercise**,	simple present I **am** thirsty.
	when conditions and results are real or possible	simple present If I **exercise**,	*will* + simple future I **will lose** weight.
SECOND CONDITIONAL	in present or future unreal conditions	simple past If I **exercised**,	*would* + simple present I **would be** healthier now.
THIRD CONDITIONAL	for unreal past events and hypothetical results	past perfect If I **had run** faster,	*would have* + past participle I **would have won** the race.

Use the phrases to write conditional sentences.

1 FIRST CONDITIONAL (present): dog listens carefully / recognizes footsteps in another room

_____

_____

2 FIRST CONDITIONAL (future): we are late / take the bus

_____

_____

3 SECOND CONDITIONAL: we improve our senses / more aware of pollution

_____

_____

! Use what you learned about conditional sentences when you prepare assignments.

4 THIRD CONDITIONAL: people developed a dog's hearing / their brains adapted

_____

_____

VOCABULARY BUILD 2

A. Below are words from the Academic Word List that you will find in Listening 2. Highlight the words you understand and then circle the words you use.

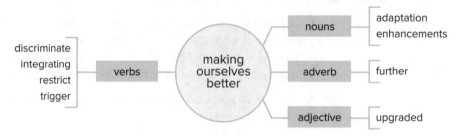

discriminate
integrating
restrict
trigger — verbs

making ourselves better

nouns — adaptation / enhancements

adverb — further

adjective — upgraded

B. Fill in the blanks with the correct words to complete the paragraph. Use a dictionary for words you don't understand.

further	integrating	restrict	trigger

In terms of _____ technology into the human body, many

people want to go _____ than just correcting disabilities.

However, some worry that this might _____ a race among

militaries to build soldiers with enhanced abilities. For this reason, many consider

that governments should _____ research in these areas.

C. Choose the word that best completes each sentence. Key words are in bold.

1 Because the building was **upgraded**, everything worked (better / worse).

2 The evolutionary **adaptation** of (decreased / improved) vision helped the eagle to hunt.

3 In trying to **discriminate** between different sounds, the dog can identify (differences / similarities).

4 In terms of **enhancements**, most people would prefer (improved / reduced) vision.

D. VOCABULARY EXTENSION: The *re-* prefix in the word *restrict* means "again" or "back." Write a definition for each of these *re-* words from Listening 2.

1 reactions (n.): _____

2 regain (v.): _____

3 relies (v.): _____

4 replace (v.): _____

5 repositioning (v.): _____

6 research (n.): _____

LISTENING ②   Our Better Selves

Mikhail Bulgakov's (1891–1940) satirical 1925 novel, *Heart of a Dog*, tells the story of a stray dog that is given human organs and certain injections and develops into a beastly man. Today, scientists are active in research to give humans biological and technological enhancements that are common among animals. While we might eventually extend our abilities and senses, we might also find that our changes in perceptions affect the ways we think, perhaps altering what it means to be human. Listening 2 reflects on what having the sensory abilities of different animals might be like.

Before You Listen

A. Write some ways in which people currently try to improve their health and fitness. Which do you think are the most effective? Discuss in a group.

_____

_____

B. Speculation—imagining the future—plays a large part in Listening 2. Read this excerpt and then write other tools we already use that extend our senses and abilities. Discuss your answers with a partner.

> But today, I'd like to branch out from the practical to the speculative and engage you with a number of "what if" questions to do with enhancing your senses. Of course, we can already enhance our senses with technology. For example, we can see both farther *and* closer with binoculars and microscopes. We can use microphones to hear the faintest sounds across great distances. We have machines in development that can smell cancer in a person and others that can analyze textures too fine for a finger to distinguish. But what if some of these technologies could be incorporated directly into the human body?

_____

_____

_____

C. These words and phrases will help you understand Listening 2. Choose the best definition for each.

1. acutely
   a) intensely
   b) attractively

2. differently abled
   a) with physical or mental challenges
   b) with enhanced abilities

3. infrared
   a) invisible light emitted by heated objects
   b) colour popular in the fashion industry

4. pattern recognition
   a) computer function for mapping data
   b) computer function for mapping camouflage

5. prosthesis
   a) sports essay
   b) artificial limb

6. spectrum
   a) rainbow or other light system
   b) range of degrees

7. speculative
   a) imagining without a basis in knowledge
   b) creating or improving one's vision

8. ultraviolet light
   a) type of blue radiation used in the creation of food colours
   b) invisible form of light that, in excess, can cause cancer

While You Listen

D. In her lecture, Dr. Morris talks about several creatures with different sensory abilities (vision, hearing, smell, taste, touch). Before you listen, reflect on what you already know about the senses of each creature. The first time you listen, take notes on each creature's abilities. Listen a second time to fill in details. Listen a third time to check your notes.

CREATURES	NOTES
EAGLES	With an eagle's vision, you could read the small print on a newspaper from 30 metres.
ELEPHANTS / PIGEONS	
CATS / MOTHS	
DOGS	

CREATURES	NOTES
AFRICAN RATS	
JEWEL BEETLES	
MOLES	

After You Listen

E. Indicate whether these statements are true or false, according to the listening.

STATEMENTS	TRUE	FALSE
1 There are machines in development to smell cancer.	☐	☐
2 People already have binoculars and microscopes in their bodies.	☐	☐
3 Cochlear implants are used to enhance a person's hearing.	☐	☐
4 Dr. Morris was called "eagle-eyed" by her father.	☐	☐
5 Most people would do an operation to have an eagle's peripheral vision.	☐	☐
6 Hearing dozens of conversations is something people already do.	☐	☐
7 Artists have a greater awareness of colour than non-artists.	☐	☐
8 A mole uses its sense of smell to detect an earthworm.	☐	☐

F. Answer these questions. Then, discuss with a partner.

1 If you could choose to improve one sense, which one would it be? Why? In your answer, reference Dr. Morris's speech.

_____

_____

2 Why might having eagle eyes influence your thinking? How would this happen?

_____

_____

③ Why does Dr. Morris think better hearing might make a more polite society? Do you agree or disagree? Explain why.

_____

_____

_____

Pronunciation: Sometimes, "the" is pronounced "thee" (to indicate it's the only one) and "a" is pronounced "eh." Use these pronunciations for emphasis.

④ Dr. Morris suggests that better senses might make us a more caring species. What does she mean by this? Do you agree or disagree? Explain why.

_____

_____

_____

Academic
Survival Skill

Paraphrasing and Summarizing

An important comprehension and study skill is discussing lectures and other types of talks (e.g., debates, interviews, speeches) after you listen to them. Discussing a lecture helps you to check whether you understood the information exactly as others did and to figure out the answers to any questions you might have had. Discussions also help you to reinforce the ideas.

Paraphrasing

One technique for capturing ideas when you listen is to paraphrase. When you paraphrase, look for the main ideas and write or say them in your own words. Start by considering what information is unessential.

A. Read this excerpt from Listening 2. Cross out the unnecessary words.

> If you implanted eagle eyes, how would it influence your thinking? You would certainly take in far greater quantities of information. Would your brain be able to process it? I would say yes; the brain is a very flexible organ. Your awareness—and I suppose your interest—in the world would increase. Artists, for example, have a greater awareness and memory for colour than non-artists.

B. Use the main ideas that you were left with in task A to write a one-sentence paraphrase of the paragraph. Compare your paraphrase with a partner's.

_____

_____

_____

Summarizing

Summarizing is not just a skill you use after listening; it's best to mentally summarize while you listen. When you hear the title or topic sentence of a presentation, you begin to get an idea of what it is about and can then choose an appropriate graphic organizer to help you summarize the ideas. You could choose a timeline for a discussion of events or a flow chart for a talk about a process. While you continue to listen, adjust your mental summary by modifying what you think based on the new information you hear.

▶

After you listen, it's easier to summarize based on notes you took while you listened. When you summarize, stick to the main points and try to identify the argument or thesis in what you heard.

C. Choose the best summary of Listening 2. Then, write an explanation of what makes it superior to the others.

- ☐ Seeing like an eagle or having a mole's sense of touch would require impractical surgical procedures that would turn people into freaks.
- ☐ Various creatures have enhanced or different senses that many people some day may be able to adopt but which might change the way they think.
- ☐ Understanding the world from another creature's point of view would not be worth the difficulty of adopting one or more new senses.

_____

_____

_____

WARM-UP ASSIGNMENT
Summarize an Interview

In this Warm-Up Assignment, you will write a summary of Listening 1 and then present it to a group of classmates.

A. Review the notes you took for Listening 1 and the answers you wrote to the questions in task E (pages 116–117).

B. Use this information to write a one-paragraph summary. Apply what you learned about summarizing in Academic Survival Skill. Write at least one conditional sentence (see Focus on Grammar, page 117).

C. Convert your notes to a graphic organizer such as a flow chart, mind map or timeline. Use your graphic organizer when you present your summary to your group.

D. Form groups of six, and present your summary to your group members.

E. When all group members have presented, ask for feedback on how you could improve your summary, graphic organizer and presentation.

VOCABULARY BUILD 3

A. Below are words and phrases from the Academic Word List that you will find in Listening 3. Highlight the words you understand and then circle the words you use.

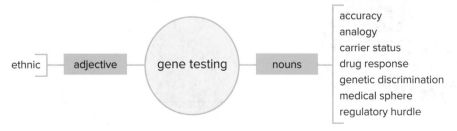

ethnic — adjective — gene testing — nouns —
accuracy
analogy
carrier status
drug response
genetic discrimination
medical sphere
regulatory hurdle

B. These phrases are medical terms. Write the correct term next to its definition.

carrier status	drug response	genetic discrimination	medical sphere

DEFINITIONS	MEDICAL TERMS
1 area within which discussions on health and wellness are likely to take part	
2 likelihood that a medicine will react differently with different people	
3 person who has bits of DNA that might give them a pass on a disease or genetic trait	
4 treating people differently based on knowing something about their DNA (e.g., employer refusing to hire someone)	

C. Draw an arrow (↓) to indicate where in each sentence the word or phrase in parentheses should be placed.

1 (accuracy) The report lacked because it did not include the patients' ages.

2 (analogy) As an comparing the human body to nature was not convincing.

3 (regulatory hurdle) The new drug faced a when it was found to cause headaches in some patients.

4 (ethnic) Many diseases are more common to people of a particular background.

Visit My eLab to complete Vocabulary Review exercises for this chapter.

LISTENING ③ **Mapping Your Chromosomes**

You probably already know a fair amount about your chromosomes, the information in each cell that helps to determine your physical appearance and characteristics. From a young age, you may have been told you have your mother's eyes or your father's hands. But beyond the visible signs of how we are related to our ancestors are the genetic markers for diseases and conditions. If several of your relatives have suffered from a disease, would you want to know if you might get it as well? In Listening 3, Amanda Lang questions Anne Wojcicki about 23andMe, a genetic testing service that could give you the answers.

Before You Listen

A. What might be the pros and cons (advantages and disadvantages) of knowing your genetic markers, especially those related to diseases that you were likely to get?

PROS	CONS

B. Read this excerpt from Listening 3. Pinpointing ethnic backgrounds and locating unknown relatives sometimes reveals information that can be uncomfortable, such as adult children discovering they were adopted. In other cases, people might find that their ethnic background is different than what they had always assumed. Would you want to know such information? Why or why not? Discuss with a partner.

> You, me and every other human being have one thing in common: twenty-three pairs of chromosomes. Those chromosomes hold millions of variations that make us all quite different. A California company is offering to map them. That would help measure someone's risk of dozens of diseases, pinpoint their ethnic background or even find an unknown relative.

C. These words and phrases will help you understand Listening 3. Match each to its definition.

WORDS/PHRASES		DEFINITIONS
1 cystic fibrosis	_____	a) spit
2 genotyping	_____	b) able to be repeated in an experiment
3 oncology	_____	c) operation to remove the breast and nearby tissues
4 pharma companies	_____	d) determining an individual's DNA
5 prophylactic	_____	e) branch of medicine that deals with cancerous tumours
6 radical mastectomy	_____	f) feeling of discomfort
7 reproducible	_____	g) companies that manufacture medical drugs
8 saliva	_____	h) intended to prevent disease
9 squeamishness	_____	i) disease that affects the lungs and other organs

While You Listen

D. Before you listen, read Lang's interview questions and think about what Wojcicki's answers might be. The first time you listen, try to get the gist of the interview. Listen a second time and take notes on the answers to the questions. Listen a third time to check your notes and add details. You will use your notes to write a summary for discussion in the Final Assignment.

LANG'S QUESTIONS	WOJCICKI'S ANSWERS
I started by asking how it works.	gives individuals their genetic information

LANG'S QUESTIONS	WOJCICKI'S ANSWERS
And what makes this possible? What's the technology that you're using that allows you to give us this detailed information?	
And what kind of information? When you say "welcome to you," what am I finding out about me?	
In the US, you've hit a kind of regulatory hurdle, with the FDA there saying, you know, "this isn't approved." What's the issue there? What are they kind of, why are they throwing up a block to this project?	Federal Drug Administration (FDA) believes …
Is there any concern about the accuracy of the information? If I get all this information, do I need to worry that it may not be true or right?	
You must've been asked many times about the kind of ethics around having this kind of information, wanting to know it. What's your response? I mean, because people have a sort of squeamishness around knowing things that maybe we shouldn't know.	cholesterol test analogy:
So, like a cholesterol test, could it be used by an insurance company against me, to make it harder for me to get some forms of insurance?	
One of the things that people have to deal with when they have information—we've seen this with the so-called breast cancer gene—is that they then may take actions, not just changing the way you eat, *à la* high cholesterol, but you know, radical mastectomy ahead of a possible diagnosis of breast cancer. Do you worry about that kind of outcome, that people will take kind of drastic steps with this information?	BRC variant associated with breast cancer American Society of Clinical Oncology recommends …
You have a vision that goes beyond just individuals having this information: the collection of a sort of bulk of data. What do you hope to do with that? Where does that get us?	

After You Listen

E. Explain the importance of these terms from Wojcicki's answers.

1 What is the meaning of the phrase "welcome to you" that people receive with their DNA results?

_____

_____

2 Why would people want to know "where they came from in the world"?

_____

_____

③ Would being a carrier of a disease like cystic fibrosis that "you're eventually going to pass down to your children" affect your decision to have children? Why or why not?

_____

_____

④ How would having your genetic information publicly available make a difference?

_____

_____

⑤ The company 23andMe wants to use people's genetic information in other ways. How?

_____

_____

F. Some diseases are largely preventable if, for example, you make good diet and fitness choices. However, others are not. Would you want to know if you were more likely than the average person to get a disease for which there was no prevention and no cure? Why or why not? Use what you have learned in Listening 3 to discuss in a group.

FOCUS ON SPEAKING

Speaking with Aids

When you listen to a lecture, it is natural to remember more if the speaker uses aids. This is because the information will be stored in different parts of your brain associated with vision, hearing and language. Such aids come in many forms, including physical objects (called *props*), visual aids like computer presentations, interactive graphics (e.g., charts that change on the screen), photos, illustrations and graphic organizers. Audio segments and video clips are also useful aids.

A. Imagine you are giving a presentation on activity trackers. Number these aids in terms of how effective you think each would be in helping your listeners to remember the content of your talk (1 = most helpful; 7 = least helpful).

_____ audience volunteer helping you demonstrate an activity tracker

_____ audio recording of a favourable testimonial from an activity tracker user

_____ chart showing an increase in the number of activity tracker users by month

_____ interactive graphics showing weight loss

_____ speaking on your own, without any aids

_____ text-only computer presentations

_____ video of a person using an activity tracker throughout the day

Among the most popular visual aids are computer presentations. The individual screens of a computer presentation are called *slides* and the collection is called a *deck*. When creating a deck, consider these points:

- Use large, readable text, but keep it to a minimum: use phrases, not full sentences.
- Make sure your slides are readable, particularly the charts and diagrams. Simplify those: include only essential information.
- Use slides to make your audience think; include questions on the slides and provide explanations as you talk.
- Use colours and memorable images to capture attention and to support your message. Avoid humour or other elements that might distract.
- When you present, never face the screen while you are speaking and don't read from it. The audience can read faster than you can speak, so add to what you have written with new information.
- Include one or two slides per minute of the lecture: too many slides lead to confusion and too few lead to boredom.

B. With a partner, discuss these three computer presentation slides about motivation. Which would make the greatest impact in your presentation?

Winston Churchill said, "If you're going through hell, keep going."

Why?

motivation (n.): reason or reasons one has for acting or behaving in a particular way

FINAL ASSIGNMENT
Participate in a Group Discussion

Use what you learned in this chapter to take part in a group discussion of the interview you heard in Listening 3.

A. Prepare for the discussion by writing a summary of the interview using the notes you took for Listening 3. If you refer to the interview questions, make sure you paraphrase. Apply what you learned about paraphrasing and summarizing in Academic Survival Skill (page 122). Write at least one conditional sentence (see Focus on Grammar, page 117).

B. On a separate page, prepare a graphic organizer, such as a flow chart, mind map or timeline, to support your summary.

C. Write three questions you would like to discuss about something you heard in the interview. For example: would people want to know if they were adopted, and what would they do with such information?

1 _____

2 _____

3 _____

D. Form a group of six and begin the discussion. During the discussion, share your summary and your graphic organizer and ask your questions. Take notes on other students' ideas. At the end, summarize what the group discussed using one visual aid (see Focus on Speaking, page 127). For example, you could use a computer-aided presentation and include the main points, possibly using a graphic organizer.

E. Choose one group member to present the summary of your discussion to the rest of the class.

F. When all groups have presented, ask for feedback on how you could improve your presentation.

How confident
are you?

Think about what you learned in this chapter. Use the table to decide what you should review.

I LEARNED ...	I AM CONFIDENT	I NEED TO REVIEW
vocabulary related to health and fitness;	☐	☐
how to predict and infer while listening;	☐	☐
about conditional sentences;	☐	☐
how to paraphrase and summarize;	☐	☐
how to use aids when speaking;	☐	☐
how to participate in a group discussion.	☐	☐

VOCABULARY
Challenge

Think about the vocabulary and ideas in this chapter. Use these words and phrases to write two sentences about the future of fitness innovations.

| accurate | analogy | discriminate | medical sphere | restrict | underestimate |

_____

_____

_____

_____

_____

_____

My eLab ✎
Visit My eLab to build on what you learned.

CHAPTER 7

New Ways to Learn

Summerhill, a British school founded in 1921, made class attendance voluntary and gave every teacher and student an equal vote in all decisions. Countless other educational experiments have sought better ways to teach and learn. Recently, technology has changed the nature of schools, partly reflecting the shift from traditional jobs requiring manual labour to new jobs that set thinking skills as a priority. In some educational contexts, the computer has become an interactive tutor, replacing the teacher, while other schools have gone in the opposite direction, rejecting technology and returning to traditional classroom practices.

What do you think is the best way to learn?

In this chapter, you will

- learn vocabulary related to education;

- listen for rhythm in sentences;

- review gerunds and infinitives;

- enhance your message with non-verbal communication;

- give a process presentation;

- write a thesis statement to start a discussion;

- take part in a group discussion.

GEARING UP

A. Look at this illustration of a traditional classroom and then answer the questions.

A Paris magazine illustration of an 1845 classroom

1 In what ways is the 1845 classroom similar to classrooms of today?

_____

_____

2 In what ways is it different?

_____

_____

3 Why have some things changed a great deal in education?

_____

_____

4 Why have some things not changed much?

_____

_____

B. Discuss the questions and your answers, first with a partner, then in a group.

FOCUS ON LISTENING

Listening for Rhythm

In Focus on Speaking, Chapter 2, page 36, you learned how intonation and stress add emphasis at the word level, helping listeners understand what is important by the way certain words or parts of words are emphasized. Rhythm is how speakers draw attention to what they have to say at the sentence level, making their speech more interesting. Rhythm in speech is often compared to music.

Stress emphasis makes some words or parts of words stand out; you can do this by pronouncing them louder or longer, or by speaking at a different pitch (higher or lower). When you stress some words and syllables, you must lower the stress on others, saying them in a weaker or more relaxed way. The process of adding and taking away stress creates rhythm in your sentences.

In sentences with rhythm, content words are stressed and function words are not stressed. Content words (e.g., *school*, *enter*) carry the meaning of the sentence; without them you would not understand the sentence. Function words (e.g., *the*, *and*, *on*) are parts of grammar that don't have much meaning on their own; they serve to connect content words, showing their relationships.

> **!**
> *Focusing on content words is a good way to take notes when you listen.*

A. Read these sentences to yourself. Notice how the absence of function words or content words affects your understanding of the sentence. Now, read the original sentence aloud with a partner. Take turns stressing the content words and the function words.

ORIGINAL SENTENCE: The traditional school trained a typical student entering a factory and assumed he or she was expected to simply take orders.

CONTENT WORDS: traditional school trained typical student entering factory assumed expected simply take orders

FUNCTION WORDS: the a a and he or she was to

B. Write *C* for content words or *F* for function words for each of the following parts of speech. Then, add more example words.

PARTS OF SPEECH	CONTENT OR FUNCTION	EXAMPLE WORDS		
adjectives	_____	orange		
adverbs	_____	quickly		
articles	_____	an		
conjunctions	_____	and		
interjections	*C*	Oh!	No!	Why!
main verbs	_____	study		
negatives	*C*	doesn't		

PARTS OF SPEECH	CONTENT OR FUNCTION	EXAMPLE WORDS		
nouns	_____	university		
prepositions	_____	on		
pronouns	_____	he		
wh- words	_____	who		

C. With a partner, highlight the content words in these sentences from Listening 1. Then, practise saying each with different rhythms. Remember to stress content words by playing with speed, volume and pitch. Also, pause slightly at commas.

1. Well, a lot of kids—and probably a few adults—wore their thumbs red playing Super Mario Brothers, and while video games are spectacularly successful as home entertainment, some hope games can equally engage students as learning tools.

2. The first thing I tell you is that you have an F, and that usually—particularly if I'm speaking to freshman—gets very pained looks in return. But then I say, "Ah, but you can level up."

3. So I thought, well, what could I do, and I thought for a minute, and thought, wait a minute, you're a game designer, why not design the entire class as a game?

VOCABULARY BUILD 1

A. Below are words from the Academic Word List that you will find in Listening 1. Highlight the words you understand and then circle the words you use.

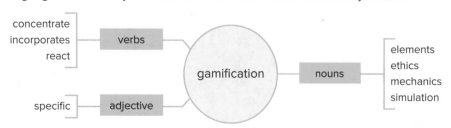

concentrate
incorporates
react — **verbs**

specific — **adjective**

gamification

nouns — elements
ethics
mechanics
simulation

B. Fill in the blanks with the correct words to complete the paragraph. Use a dictionary to look up words you don't understand.

ethics	incorporates	react	specific

A society generally _____ a set of beliefs about how people

should behave. We call this set of beliefs _____, and these

are built around how the society views _____ problems.

Sometimes a society faces a new problem and an individual has to

_____ in a way that considers how the set of beliefs applies.

C. Choose the word or phrase that best completes each sentence. Key words are in bold.

① It's often necessary to **concentrate** on the small details of a problem.

    a) ponder   b) improve   c) focus

② There are many **elements** that go into making a classroom successful.

    a) parts   b) hot points   c) chemicals

③ A board game **simulation** of a stock market won't involve real money.

    a) investment   b) introduction   c) imitation

④ Traditional **mechanics** may not have the skills to repair new cars' electric systems.

    a) robots   b) repair personnel   c) computers

D. VOCABULARY EXTENSION: The Latin *corp* in *incorporates* refers to *body* and is used in words like *corps* (group of people) and *corpse* (dead body). Based on the meaning of the Latin roots in the table, write definitions for the words.

LATIN ROOT	MEANING	WORDS AND DEFINITIONS
cardi-	heart	cardiograph:
corp-	body	corporation:
manu-	hand	manual:
or-	mouth	orifice:
ped-	foot	pedicure:

Beyond entertainment, games for the young are often about learning skills that will be useful later in life. Today, many video games teach competitive and collaborative strategies, political systems and money management. Could games be used to improve the teaching of subjects in a university context? Listening 1 explores this question in an interview with Professor Lee Sheldon, who talks about how he uses game-based learning in his classes.

Before You Listen

A. One focus of Listening 1 is the idea of motivation. Motivation is usually either *intrinsic* (based on personal interest or desires) or *extrinsic* (based on external pressures). For example, students may play a game for pure enjoyment (intrinsic) or because their teacher directs them to do so (extrinsic). Write three things you do that are intrinsically motivated and three that are extrinsically motivated.

INTRINSICALLY MOTIVATED	EXTRINSICALLY MOTIVATED
❶	❶
❷	❷
❸	❸

B. Read this excerpt from Listening 1. Then, in a group, discuss which features of a video game might be included when designing a new way to teach various subjects.

> Well, a lot of kids—and probably a few adults—wore their thumbs red playing Super Mario Brothers, and while video games are spectacularly successful as home entertainment, some hope games can equally engage students as learning tools. Today, as part of our project By Design, we were looking at designing a curriculum that incorporates gaming. The buzzword in education is "gamification"; the students are studying game design and taking a course from one of gamification's pioneers.

C. These words and phrases will help you understand Listening 1. Choose the best definition for each.

❶ attrition
   a) gradually reducing strength
   b) identifying a location

❷ avatars
   a) blue aliens
   b) online representations of a person

❸ buzzword
   a) language of bees
   b) fashionable phrase

❹ clunky
   a) awkward and outdated
   b) sound of a broken wheel

❺ run of the mill
   a) ordinary
   b) unordinary

❻ sage on the stage
   a) teacher-centred
   b) learner-centred

❼ spiff up
   a) make less attractive
   b) make more attractive

While You Listen

D. Listening 1 gives perspectives on a course based on gaming principles. The first time you listen, try to understand the gist. Listen a second time and complete the notes. Listen a third time to identify the three sentences you practised in Focus on Listening, task C (page 133). Think about your use of rhythm compared to how the speakers say the sentences.

SPEAKERS	NOTES
Anna Maria Tremonti	• games can equally engage students as _____ • students studying game design course from gamification pioneer
Student 1	• we had to make a story of _____
Student 2	• competing with classmates is _____

Student 1	• incentive/motivation
	
	  – short-term and long-term _____
	
	  – not motivated by _____

Lee Sheldon	• gamification = _____ • aka: _____
	• you start class with an F but can _____ • class is designed as a game: *competition + collaboration* _____ • apply gaming principles _____
	• not letter grades: _____ • complete a quest or craft something = _____
	• research (questing) to take exams: _____ • _____ • _____
	• teaching like this since 2008
	• class maps game terminology *onto game-related activities* _____ • activities have _____ • added _____

	• benefits:
	
	  – grades: _____
	
	  – attendance _____
	
	  – make up _____
	
	  – intrinsic rather than _____
	
	  – extrinsic rewards = _____

After You Listen

E. Review your notes and number these sentences in the correct order to form a summary of Listening 1.

_____1_____ A university course on learning how to create video games is structured like a video game.

_____ Beyond creating an avatar and a game, there is an option to create your own assignments.

_____ Doing well can earn you "fat loot," such as clothes and hairstyles to enhance your avatar.

_____ Finally, attendance is not assessed.

_____ However, they can improve on this F grade by levelling up—completing tasks to improve their scores.

_____ Part of learning from your mistakes is creating an avatar, which will change over time.

_____ Part of levelling up involves researching materials (questing) to prepare for exams, but exams can be retaken to ensure you learn from your mistakes.

_____ The first unusual part of the class is that students are told that they start the class with an F grade.

F. Answer the following questions and then discuss your answers with a partner.

1 What is surprising about gamification as an approach?

_____

_____

2 Why is attendance so high in this course compared to other courses?

_____

_____

3 Why does the teacher let the students repeat the exam as often as they like?

_____

_____

4 What other subjects are being taught using gamification?

_____

_____

5 Why do students enter the class with an F grade?

_____

_____

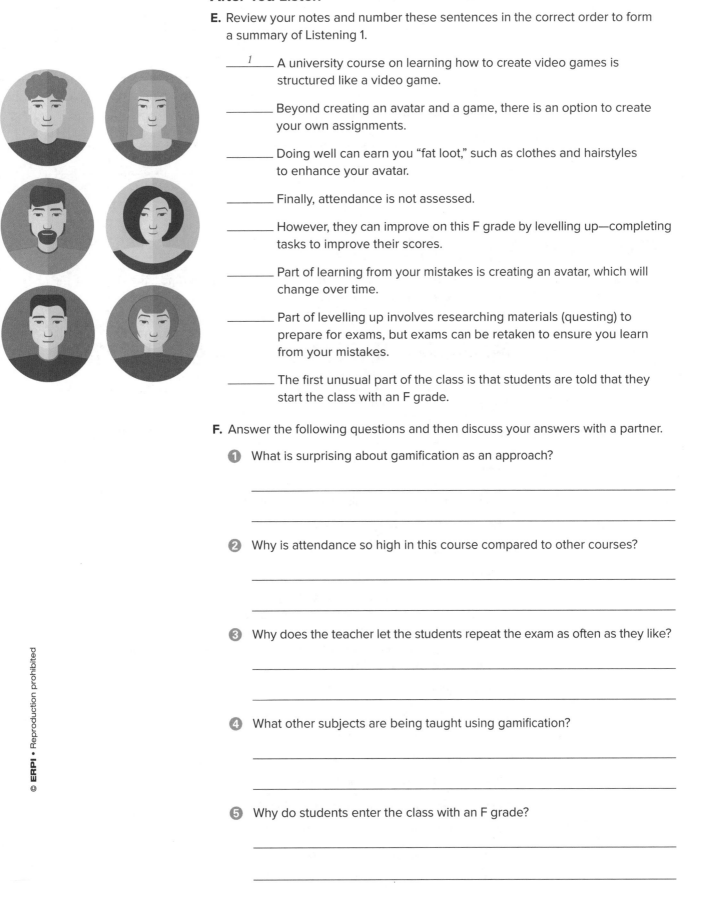

6 Why does the teacher use gamification rather than a traditional approach?

_____

_____

7 The Holocaust—the Nazis' murder of millions during WW II—is not a light-hearted topic. What might be the pros and cons of teaching serious topics as games? Discuss in a group.

_____

_____

_____

FOCUS ON GRAMMAR

Gerunds and Infinitives

When you listened to Listening 1, you may have noticed gerunds, the -ing form of the verb. _Gerunds_ and _infinitives_ are verb forms that act like nouns. They can be the subject, object or complement of the subject.

PART OF SENTENCE	GERUND	INFINITIVE
subject	**Reading** is fun.	**To read** is fun.*
object	I like **reading**.	I like **to read**.
complement	Something I love is **reading**.	Something I love is **to read**.

*Expressions using the infinitive as the subject are considered formal and uncommon in casual speech and writing.

Gerunds and infinitives can also have subjects and objects:

Reading **a book** is fun. I like to read **a book**.

Like other nouns, gerunds (but not infinitives) can be modified by adjectives:

Bedtime reading is fun.

In some cases, such as with the verb _like_, you can use either a gerund or an infinitive. However, sometimes the choice of a gerund or an infinitive depends on the main verb of the sentence. There are many gerunds and infinitives; pay attention when you listen and read to learn when to use each one. Here are some rules and commonly used gerunds and infinitives.

Use a gerund:

• When you use a form of _go_ with sporting activities and pastimes:

She **went** _swimming_. He **goes** _shopping_.

• After a preposition, as the object:

We'll eat **before** _starting_ our homework.

• When you use expressions with _have_, _spend_ and _waste_:

We **spent** the day _reading_. I **wasted** my time _sleeping_.

• When you describe a concrete action:

I **like** _teaching_.

▶

Use an infinitive:

• When you show intention or purpose:

　I **want** *to teach*. I **will** study *to improve*.

• When you show a reason:

　We **were glad** *to see* their progress.

• When you talk about a general or possible action:

　I **would like** *to learn*.

• When the verb is followed by a pronoun or noun referring to a person:

　I asked **him** *to study*.

A. These verbs are usually followed by a gerund. Write sentences for each combination of verbs. Use any tense for the first verb and change the second verb into a gerund.

1. appreciate + see: *I appreciate seeing old friends.* _____

　_____

2. complete + watch: _____

　_____

3. discuss + donate: _____

　_____

4. involve + try: _____

　_____

5. suggest + find: _____

　_____

B. These verbs are usually followed by an infinitive. Write sentences for each combination of verbs. Use any tense for the first verb and change the second verb into an infinitive.

1. agree + fight: *The group agreed not to fight the new proposal.* _____

　_____

2. decide + move: _____

　_____

3. learn + program: _____

　_____

4. need + repeat: _____

　_____

5. plan + arrive: _____

　_____

!

Use what you learned about gerunds and infinitives when you prepare assignments.

FOCUS ON SPEAKING

Enhancing your Message with Non-verbal Communication

Why is it you sometimes have difficulty understanding what people mean when they text or phone? The problem may have to do with a lack of visual clues: facial expressions or body language. When you speak, you use a mixture of posture (how you stand), facial expressions and hand gestures.

A. Look at these different facial expressions and hand gestures. Then, write the idea or emotion that the man is trying to express in each. Compare answers with a partner.

IDEA OR EMOTION EXPRESSED

1 _____ **2** _____ **3** _____

4 _____ **5** _____ **6** _____

7 _____ **8** _____ **9** _____

B. Practise reading this excerpt from Listening 1 with a partner. The first time, read it aloud with no expressions or gestures. Without looking at the words, try saying it a second time with facial expressions and gestures; it does not matter if you do not capture the exact words.

> So, my character, her name was Hipster, and her backstory is that she grew up in this island, her mom and dad were mechanics or engineers, and other people made up their avatars and you need to create a story to intermix them together. I was like the mechanic, someone else was a thief, and someone else was a whatever, and then we had to make a story of how they work together and how they met each other and that was what we built upon.

C. Discuss how your presentation with facial expressions and gestures added to the message you were trying to share.

When speaking, be careful of your hand gestures; what is common in one culture may be rude in another.

A. Below are words and phrases from the Academic Word List that you will find in Listening 2. Highlight the words you understand and then circle the words you use.

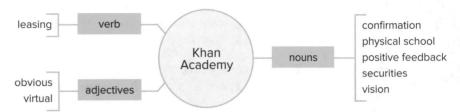

leasing — verb

obvious
virtual — adjectives

Khan
Academy

nouns —
confirmation
physical school
positive feedback
securities
vision

B. Choose the word or phrase in parentheses that best completes each sentence. Key words are in bold.

1. In order to give a lot of **positive feedback**, the teacher (praised / criticized) the students.

2. Because of his job, he couldn't attend a **physical school** so he studied (at college / online).

3. He had a **vision** of what the new university might do (differently / in the same way).

4. As a **virtual** assistant, the computer program did (real-world / computer-based) tasks.

C. Choose the best definition for each word. Use a dictionary to check your answers.

1. confirmation — a) blessing — b) approval

2. leasing — a) renting — b) selling

3. obvious — a) unclear — b) evident

4. securities — a) documents in place of money — b) strong police presence

LISTENING ②   Khan Academy

In November 2013, Khan Academy had more than ten million users per month who were completing approximately four million learning problems a day. It was an enormous impact for a school that only had forty-nine employees and offered its courses for free.

Founder Sal Khan says that his goal is to provide a world-class education for anyone, anywhere. For his work, he has been called a superstar teacher. However, surprisingly, Khan has no background in education. Listening 2 explains how Khan Academy got its start.

Before You Listen

A. Khan Academy offers instructional videos on math and other subjects that let students learn at their own pace, spending longer on topics they find difficult and progressing more quickly on those they find easy. Why would this work well online but not in a traditional classroom? What are the benefits? What are the drawbacks? Discuss with a partner and decide what topics you might like to learn through online tutorials.

B. This excerpt from Listening 2 explains the beginnings of Khan Academy. Which skills and what steps would have been necessary for Khan to turn his private tutorials into what might become the world's largest school?

> If we rewind back to 2004, that's when I was an analyst at an investment firm, my cousin in New Orleans needed help. I lived in Boston. I just started working with her remotely, but that was just one cousin remotely tutoring another cousin after work and after school for her. Now we're in the fall of 2006, word had gotten around in the family that free tutoring was going on, so now I found myself every day after work working with about ten or fifteen kids, getting on the phone, etcetera, etcetera.

_____

_____

_____

C. These words and phrases will help you understand Listening 2. Match each to its definition.

WORDS/PHRASES		DEFINITIONS
❶ backhandedly	_____	a) promoting something with enthusiasm
❷ evangelizing	_____	b) innocent
❸ footage	_____	c) available in a phone directory
❹ listed	_____	d) compliment that could be considered insulting
❺ literally	_____	e) video clips
❻ naive	_____	f) investing based on predicting a stock will fall
❼ no-brainer	_____	g) exactly as said
❽ push the envelope	_____	h) something that is easily decided
❾ shorting	_____	i) try something

While You Listen

D. Sal Khan mentions several people and organizations and the roles they played in helping the Khan Academy become a success. The first time you listen, take notes on each person or group's involvement. The second time you listen, notice Khan's facial expressions and body language as he tells his story. Listen a third time to check facts and add details.

PERSON OR GROUP	INVOLVEMENT
cousin in New Orleans (2004)	
ten or fifteen kids (2006)	
friend suggested an idea	
cousins' feedback	
people who were not his cousins (summer 2007)	
Khan and his wife	
Ann Doerr	
	found out Khan wasn't supporting himself; donated
six kids	
twenty kids	
Doerr	sends e-mails from the Aspen Festival
Bill Gates	on stage talking about Khan Academy
Gates with (author) Walter Isaacs	
Larry Cohen, Gates' chief of staff (August 2010)	

PERSON OR GROUP	INVOLVEMENT
Google (summer 2010)	Hey, what do you want to do? What are you doing?
Google engineers and executives	
Khan tells Gates	free education for anyone, anywhere; translate videos; interactive; dashboards for teachers
Gates Foundation and Google	

After You Listen

E. Indicate whether these statements are true or false, according to the listening.

STATEMENTS	TRUE	FALSE
❶ Khan was working at an investment firm when he started tutoring.	☐	☐
❷ His cousins were living in Boston at the time.	☐	☐
❸ His cousins told others who became interested in being tutored.	☐	☐
❹ Khan's cousins put some of his videos up on YouTube.	☐	☐
❺ Khan and his wife had been saving for a house.	☐	☐
❻ Khan's decision to use savings meant he could quit his job.	☐	☐
❼ Khan Academy was sold to Google for millions of dollars.	☐	☐
❽ Khan's vision includes translating Khan Academy into many languages.	☐	☐

F. Read the following points. Explain why each was important to the creation of the Khan Academy.

❶ living in a different city than his cousins: _____

_____

❷ putting a few videos up on YouTube: _____

_____

❸ coming to the attention of Ann Doerr: _____

_____

❹ having Bill Gates talk about Khan Academy publicly: _____

_____

❺ meeting with Gates and Google: _____

_____

G. Here are examples of Khan using gerunds and infinitives. In the blank spaces, rewrite the sentences. Change the gerund forms into infinitive forms, or the infinitive form into a gerund.

GERUND	INFINITIVE
Word had gotten around in the family that free **tutoring** was going on.	
	She wanted to meet.
One kid invented shorting on his own.	

WARM-UP ASSIGNMENT
Give a Process Presentation

How do you make spaghetti? How was the first rocket invented? You often have to explain how to do something or how something was done in the past. These are examples of *processes*. Listening 1 talked about the process of adapting gaming principles to teaching different subjects. Listening 2 talked about the process involved in creating the Khan Academy, beginning with the first step of helping a few kids with their homework. In this Warm-Up Assignment, you will explain a process you used to learn a new skill.

A. Choose a topic. Select something you learned that required several steps, for example, how to play a game, musical instrument or sport, or a skill related to a job. Ask your teacher for approval of your topic.

B. Use this format and organize your presentation on a separate page.

STEPS IN THE PROCESS	WHAT TO SAY
Introduce yourself and your topic.	Hello, my name is _____. Today, I'd like to explain the process of learning to _____.
Present the process in a logical order. Use transition words to signal the steps.	The process of learning to _____ involves _____ steps. The first step ... The next step ... Then, ... Finally, ...
Conclude with a summary. Explain where further information is available, and ask for questions.	In summary, learning to _____ is as easy as _____, _____ and _____. If you are interested in learning to _____, you can find more information (online/at the library/by talking to ...). Do you have any questions?

C. Practise your presentation with a partner. Use both body language (see Focus on Speaking, page 140) and rhythm (Focus on Listening, page 132). Make sure you use gerunds and infinitives correctly. Ask for feedback from your partner.

D. Present to the class. Ask your teacher and classmates for feedback on what could be improved. In the Final Assignment, your presentation or that of another student will form the basis of an academic discussion.

A. Below are words and phrases from the Academic Word List that you will find in Listening 3. Highlight the words you understand and then circle the words you use.

classic — adjective

education — nouns — appreciation / assumption / ideology / liberal arts

advocate / clarify / reinforce — verbs

B. Write short definitions for these words and phrase. Use a dictionary if needed.

1 advocate: _____

2 assumption: _____

3 classic: _____

4 liberal arts: _____

Pronunciation: With new words, learn the difference between the stress on the verb "advocate" (long a) and the noun "advocate" (short a).

C. Fill in the blanks with the words that have the closest meaning to the words and phrases in bold.

appreciation	clarify	ideology	reinforce

1 It was necessary to **strengthen** (_____) the walls before the hurricane.

2 His **system of beliefs** (_____) was based on relying on your own resources.

3 They wanted to express their **thanks** (_____) for his gifts to the school.

4 I listened to a recording to **make certain of** (_____) what the professor meant.

My eLab ✎

Visit My eLab to complete Vocabulary Exercises for this chapter.

LISTENING ③

Three Approaches to Education

Education has been called "a history of untried hypotheses." This means that new ideas of how to teach and learn have been constantly introduced but not properly tested in a way that would show how one was superior to another. Many schools once trained students to enter factory-style jobs where they were simply expected to take orders. But the nature of work is shifting and future jobs might be quite different when students graduate. In Listening 3, heads of three educational programs describe their perspectives on what is important in education.

Before You Listen

A. The composer John Cage (1912–1992) criticized college education as being about two hundred people reading the same book when two hundred people could read two hundred books. His point was that the traditional education system encourages everyone to think alike rather than giving them the chance

to think differently and then compare individual ideas. If we followed Cage's advice, how would a college literature course with students reading two hundred different books work?

_____

_____

B. Read this excerpt from Listening 3. Based on what Sam Ashworth says, explain why he might use the phrase, "I'm not ashamed to say." What might this expression suggest about the other two schools being represented in this discussion?

> I'm Sam Ashworth, head of The New Academy, a liberal arts college that prepares learners for the future by exploring classic works of rhetoric, literature and logic. This takes place in small seminars where students are encouraged to reflect, think and debate the great issues of our time. All students at The New Academy learn Latin and Greek, as well as the social sciences: psychology, sociology, law—that sort of thing. I'm not ashamed to say that a student from two hundred years ago would find the school quite familiar; we advocate—and build on—the best of what has worked in the past.

_____

_____

_____

C. These words will help you understand Listening 3. Fill in the blanks with the correct words to complete each sentence. Look up words you don't understand in a dictionary.

adversity	artificial	comradeship	nurturing	rhetoric	stamina

① The art of _____ includes techniques to help you argue, persuade and motivate.

② Sports help promote _____, or friendship among students.

③ Physical tasks that take _____ help build strength and character.

④ Teachers have a _____ role that lets them bring out the best in students.

⑤ Doing tasks that are not likely to be done in the real world is

_____.

⑥ We all face _____ in the form of challenges that must be overcome.

While You Listen

D. Listening 3 is a discussion between heads of three different educational programs. Read the categories in the table that will compare what each speaker has to say about their school. The first time you listen, try to get the general idea of how the schools differ. The second time you listen, fill in the details. Listen a third time to check your notes.

	THE NEW ACADEMY	MAPLE LAKE OUTDOOR EDUCATION CENTRE	COCOON
TYPE OF SCHOOL			computer futures centre
STRUCTURE			
PURPOSE			design a computer application
WHO ARE THE STUDENTS			
WHAT IS TAUGHT			
PHYSICAL EXERCISE			
WHAT THE STUDENTS DO AFTER			

After You Listen

E. Complete each of the following statements, according to the information in the listening. Then, discuss your answers with a partner.

1 By "nurturing the body as well as the mind," the speaker is suggesting

_____

2 The mention of "team activities" is considered _____

_____

3 When one speaker says "classrooms can seem so artificial," she probably

means _____

_____

4 Challenging students/partners is something _____

_____

5 The idea of letting students face adversity is _____

_____

6 Facing problems and figuring out an approach is seen as _____

_____

7 The phrase "prepare young people for the unknown" refers to _____

_____

F. Based on the descriptions of the three programs, which would you most like to attend and why? Discuss your preferences in a group. Support your choice with what the speaker says about the program.

Starting a Discussion with a Thesis Statement

When you have an academic discussion, as opposed to a casual conversation, you require a clear thesis, or point to be discussed. You also need evidence in the form of facts. Besides evidence, anecdotes, quotes and rhetorical questions can help support your points.

A thesis statement usually promotes discussion by comparing two things, favouring one over the other. For example:

Online dictionaries offer more than paper dictionaries.

The thesis statement must have a clear point of view and be easy to understand. It should avoid unnecessary information and have a single argument, not a mix of two or more arguments.

A. Rewrite these thesis statements to make them clearer. Then, practise saying the statements with a partner.

1 Education systems—that is, different kinds of school systems used over the course of history—have mostly been about teaching, that is, the focus has been on the teacher, not the learner, and this is wrong.

_____

_____

_____

2 When students are not doing their best, they should take responsibility for their work, and their attendance should be consistently good, to be respectful to the teacher and other students.

_____

_____

_____

3 Computers have many benefits and are also used to commit plagiarism and spread viruses.

_____

_____

Once you have a thesis, an academic discussion needs evidence. Imagine your thesis is:

As is common in a mastery-learning model, students should be able to retake exams until they achieve a perfect mark.

B. Which two of these three pieces of evidence would you use? Why? Discuss with a partner.

☐ When compared with students in traditionally taught classes, students in well-implemented mastery learning classes consistently reach higher levels of achievement and develop greater confidence in their ability to learn and in themselves as learners.

☐ Mastery learning is an instructional strategy that results in a comprehensive grasp of curriculum as demonstrated through performance-based evaluations. Teachers support student mastery of material by providing guidance and assistance.

☐ Mastery-based learning was first introduced in the 1920s through the Winnetka Plan, an educational experiment engineered by district superintendent Carleton Washburne of Winnetka, Illinois. The experiment was inspired by John Dewey's (1859–1952) research in the University of Chicago Laboratory School.

Beyond evidence, discussions often include anecdotes (short personal stories that illustrate an idea), quotations (a famous person's words that distil wisdom on the topic) and rhetorical questions, which make people think.

C. In a group, discuss the following anecdote, quotation and rhetorical question. How would each help support points in a discussion on mastery learning?

ANECDOTE: I failed to get my driver's licence three times. Each time I failed for a different reason. By the time I got it, I knew I wouldn't make those same mistakes again.

QUOTATION: Author Bram Stoker (1847–1912) said, "We learn from failure, not from success."

RHETORICAL QUESTION: If we let student doctors retake their medical exams as often as they like, is it any guarantee they will remember the information after they graduate?

FINAL ASSIGNMENT
Take Part in an Academic Discussion

Use what you learned in this chapter to take part in a group discussion about improving a learning process.

A. Form a group of six. Choose one member's topic from the Warm-Up Assignment. Write a thesis statement for discussion. Use what you learned in Academic Survival Skill. For example, your thesis statement may be something like:

The process of teaching someone to ... should be improved.

B. Ask your teacher to approve your topic and your thesis statement.

C. Prepare for your group discussion individually. Collect evidence to support your view, as well as anecdotes and relevant quotations you can use to contribute to the discussion. Think of rhetorical questions you could ask.

D. Conduct your group discussion in front of the class. When it is your turn to speak, use appropriate body language, hand gestures and facial expressions (refer to Focus on Speaking, page 140). Use stress, intonation and rhythm to add emphasis to your points (see Focus on Listening, page 132) and vary your sentences with gerunds and infinitives (review Focus on Grammar on page 138).

E. During your group discussion, listen carefully to what group members say and look for opportunities to introduce your evidence, anecdotes or quotations and to ask your rhetorical questions.

F. At the end, have one group member restate the thesis and briefly summarize the discussion.

G. As other groups present, take notes on a separate page answering these questions:

- What is the group's name and/or topic?
- Is the thesis statement clear?
- How well has the group addressed concerns in the thesis statement?
- Have the group members discussed the topic constructively, building on what each member said?
- Is the summary clear? Does it reflect what was discussed?

H. After all the groups have finished, share feedback on each group's performance.

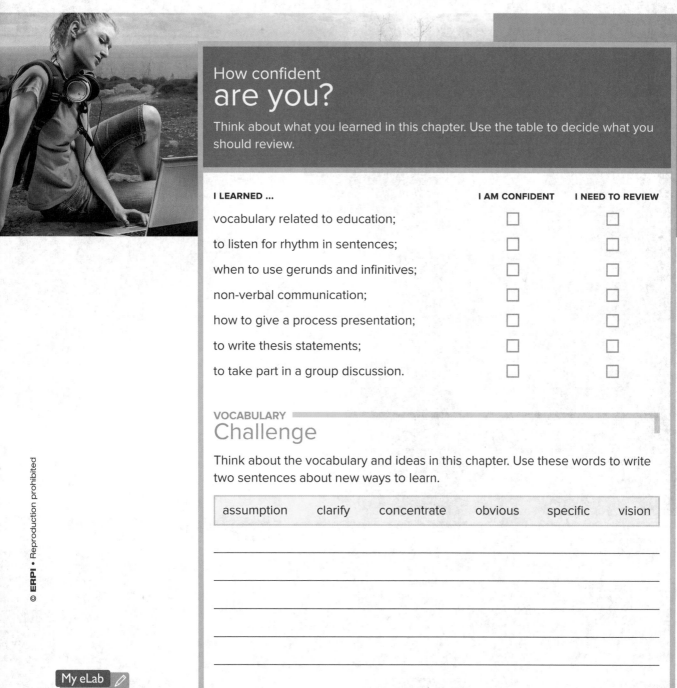

How confident
are you?

Think about what you learned in this chapter. Use the table to decide what you should review.

I LEARNED ...	I AM CONFIDENT	I NEED TO REVIEW
vocabulary related to education;	☐	☐
to listen for rhythm in sentences;	☐	☐
when to use gerunds and infinitives;	☐	☐
non-verbal communication;	☐	☐
how to give a process presentation;	☐	☐
to write thesis statements;	☐	☐
to take part in a group discussion.	☐	☐

VOCABULARY
Challenge

Think about the vocabulary and ideas in this chapter. Use these words to write two sentences about new ways to learn.

assumption	clarify	concentrate	obvious	specific	vision

_____

_____

_____

_____

_____

_____

My eLab
Visit My eLab to build on what you learned.

CHAPTER 8

Finding Justice

A 1754 BCE carving of the Code of Hammurabi is among the oldest intact set of laws. It includes the infamous punishment "an eye for an eye." Although many of the Code's punishments were brutal and long since abandoned, some aspects —considering the impact on victims for example— are being looked at in new ways today, such as through restorative justice. The legal system is also faced with modern issues: white-collar (business) crimes, computer-based crimes and questions of when identity tracking becomes an illegal intrusion on a person's privacy.

How should society deal with old and new crimes in the twenty-first century?

In this chapter,
you will

- learn vocabulary related to law and justice;

- distinguish fact from opinion;

- review modals that express possibility;

- find ways to construct an argument;

- give a persuasive presentation;

- explore debate strategies;

- participate in a debate.

GEARING UP

A. Look at the image and then answer the questions.

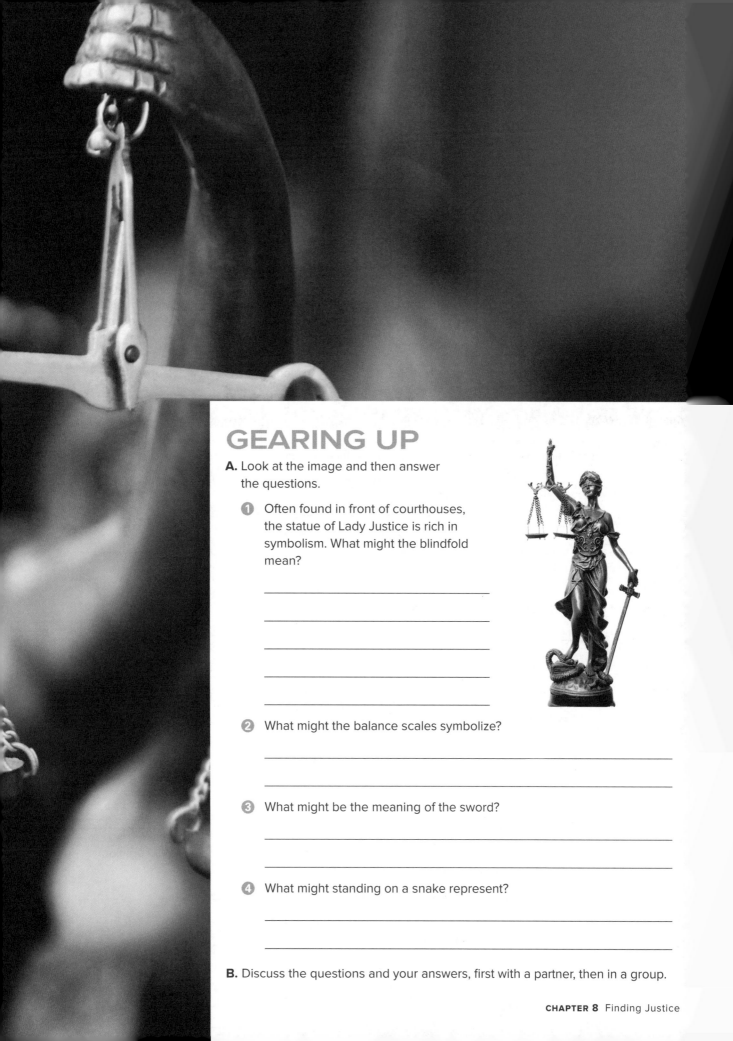

1 Often found in front of courthouses, the statue of Lady Justice is rich in symbolism. What might the blindfold mean?

_____

_____

_____

_____

_____

2 What might the balance scales symbolize?

_____

_____

3 What might be the meaning of the sword?

_____

_____

4 What might standing on a snake represent?

_____

_____

B. Discuss the questions and your answers, first with a partner, then in a group.

Distinguishing Fact from Opinion

When you listen to a speaker, you may wonder whether you are hearing facts or opinions. *Facts* are statements that are generally agreed to be true because they have been investigated or established by research and experiments. Sometimes facts are accepted after logically considering available evidence. For example, no one has been to another star system, but we can use observation, measurement and logic to understand that stars exist.

Opinions are statements that reflect what someone thinks or feels about something. For example, if someone thinks humans will never travel to another star system, that is an opinion. However, there are also valid opinions. *Valid opinions* are opinions backed by evidence. For example, if someone explains that even using the fastest of rockets, it would still take hundreds of years of travel to reach another star system and says, "It's unlikely anyone will visit another star system in the next five hundred years," then that's a *valid* opinion. You cannot argue about facts, but you can argue about opinions.

A. Read the comparisons of facts and opinions and the examples of valid opinions. Then, add other examples where needed.

QUESTIONS	FACTS	OPINIONS	EXAMPLES OF VALID OPINIONS
IS IT TRUE?	Facts are scientifically proven or agreed upon by experts. Example: _____ _____ _____	Opinions are personal beliefs that may not be shared by others. Example: *There are too many* *people in Canada's prisons.* _____	There are too many people in Canada's prisons because 41 to 44 percent of prisoners reoffend within two years.
DOES IT EXIST?	Facts can be observed first-hand by anyone. Example: *The Peel County Jail is* *now a museum.* _____	Opinions cannot be observed or supported by proof. Example: _____ _____ _____	Lots of people think jails are overcrowded because they believe the news reports.
HAS IT OCCURRED?	Even if something cannot be observed today, facts can be established by logical thought. Example: _____ _____ _____	Opinions lack evidence or scientific credibility. Example: *Ancient Greek soldiers* *had to fight monsters.* _____	Most ancient Greeks probably believed in monsters, based on _____ _____ _____

B. Indicate whether each of these statements is fact, opinion or valid opinion. Discuss your answers with a partner.

1. The legal system is far too easy on criminals. _____

2. The fifty-three local car robberies probably mean people are forgetting to lock their car doors. _____

3️⃣ Nearly two million criminal incidents were reported to Canadian police in 2012. _____

4️⃣ Crime is increasing because of violent video games and movies. _____

5️⃣ Shoplifting is a huge problem; thefts of $5000 or under (usually shoplifting) accounted for 18 percent of youth crime in 2012. _____

C. Comparative and superlative adjectives (better/best) may signal opinions, along with statements that feature phrases like "I think" or "people say." Vague words like *some* and *a few* may also signal opinions. Numerical data—statistics and dates—often indicate facts. Read these statements and highlight the words or phrases that suggest each is an opinion.

1️⃣ I've heard that white-collar criminals don't usually go to jail.

2️⃣ Other than hurting someone, identity theft is the easiest kind of crime.

3️⃣ The leader of a country can't be sent to prison while in office, or so people say.

4️⃣ Going to jail is a lot better for some people because they get food and a bed.

5️⃣ Everyone knows that stealing from a bank is worse than stealing from a store.

6️⃣ The stupidest crime anyone can commit is stealing a car.

> ❗ When you challenge someone's opinions, first try to see what facts you both agree on.

A. Below are words and phrases from the Academic Word List that you will find in Listening 1. Highlight the words you understand and then circle the words you use.

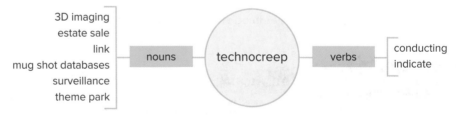

nouns — technocreep — verbs

3D imaging
estate sale
link
mug shot databases
surveillance
theme park

conducting
indicate

B. Choose the phrase that best completes each sentence. Key words are in bold.

1️⃣ To investigate privacy issues, the university is **conducting** an experiment to see _____.

   a) how much private information people give away

   b) the number of public information workers

   c) how much public information people collect

2️⃣ It's important to **indicate** your choice when _____.

   a) you are told what to do

   b) there is no reason to act

   c) you vote in an election

3 In terms of **surveillance**, the government makes use of _____.

   a) a large staff to review tax returns

   b) cameras that can identify faces

   c) window blinds and soundproof rooms

4 The **theme park** includes several _____.

   a) restaurants and parking spots

   b) rides and attractions

   c) government security officials

C. Draw an arrow (↓) to indicate where in each sentence the word or phrase in parentheses should be placed.

1 (3D imaging) The process of the heart helped identify where to operate.

2 (estate sale) After the actor's death, an was held to sell his belongings.

3 (link) There was a clear between the theft of his credit card and the purchase of a car.

4 (mug shot databases) The police used to match the criminal to the video.

 **Technocreep**

After looking up a recipe for pizza on the Internet, you suddenly find your other searches include pop-up advertisements for local Italian restaurants and flights to Italy. Everyone who has searched the Internet has had a similar experience, and it is one of the ways your privacy is being invaded by companies eager to sell goods and services. When do these kinds of activities cross the line and become illegal? In Listening 1, Tom Keenan talks about *technocreep*, the tendency for technology to creep (advance slowly) into our lives: stealing and using private information.

Before You Listen

A. Many high-technology devices now use scans of fingerprints, palms, faces or irises (part of your eye) for identification. When these are tied to your personal information, you become easy to track. What might be the dangers of sharing this kind of information? Discuss with a partner.

B. In this humorous excerpt from Listening 1, Mary takes a telephone order for a pizza from Mr. Kelly. Practise it with a partner and then discuss how it relates to concerns about privacy.

> **MARY:** Is this Mr. Kelly? I show your national identification number as 6102049998-45-54610; is that correct?
>
> **MR. KELLY:** Uh, yes. I'd like to order a couple of your double-meat special pizzas.
>
> **MARY:** There will be a new twenty-dollar charge for this, sir.
>
> **MR. KELLY:** What do you mean?
>
> **MARY:** Sir, the system shows me that your medical records indicate that you have high blood pressure and extremely high cholesterol. Luckily, we have a new agreement with your national health-care provider that allows us to sell you double-meat pies as long as you agree to wave all future claims of liability.
>
> **MR. KELLY:** What?
>
> **MARY:** Gotta watch that waist if you're hitting the beach, eh? Forty-two inches, wow. Whoa, looks like you maxed out on all your credit cards. Bring cash, OK?

C. These words and phrases will help you understand Listening 1. Match each to its definition.

WORDS/PHRASES		DEFINITIONS
❶ adjunct professor	_____	a) responsibility
❷ capitalization	_____	b) country's system of identifying citizens
❸ dovetail	_____	c) people pretending to be those who use violence politically
❹ liability	_____	d) part-time professor
❺ national ID	_____	e) radio frequency identification
❻ NSA	_____	f) finding a way to create money from something
❼ pseudo-terrorists	_____	g) fit together with
❽ RFID	_____	h) National Security Agency

While You Listen

D. Before you listen, read the interview questions on the next page. The first time you listen, try to understand the gist. Listen a second time to fill in the answers and a third time to check and add details, noting which information is opinion or fact. Ask yourself whether or not you agree with Keenan's opinions.

INTERVIEW QUESTIONS	RESPONSES AND ARGUMENT
Listening to that pizza ad, the call-in there, how far-fetched is that?	*It's real. (fact)* *The national ID number is used for all services in Estonia, but North America pushes back. (fact)* *Target/pregnant girl example (fact)*
Wow, they tracked buying habits. How did they do that?	
So, how do you define *technocreep*?	
So, we have heard for some time that technology is compromising our privacy. You say that we're actually in a new era of infiltration?	
So in other words, if they can find who bought the ticket, they can find who bought other things. They can actually link you up to lots of other things?	
What precisely are they doing?	
The American government is conducting an experiment right now called BOSS: Biometric Optical Surveillance System. Does that somehow dovetail with what you're talking about?	
So you're saying that potential for misuse is great, but who's going to do the misusing?	

After You Listen

E. Answer the following questions to better understand Keenan's arguments against technocreep.

➊ Why are stores anxious to assign a personal identification number to individual customers?

_____

_____

2 What was the Target department store's reaction after being criticized for predicting a girl was pregnant and sending her pregnancy-related advertisements?

_____

_____

3 Why does Keenan find it disturbing to shop for a chandelier, and then see Google advertisements for other chandeliers pop up?

_____

_____

4 Why is it a concern that a woman who bought a winning lottery ticket was tracked by video?

_____

_____

5 How does the Calgary Police Service use its facial recognition system?

_____

_____

6 How might videotaping people outside polling stations be used against them?

_____

_____

7 Although the use of a BOSS system is meant to identify terrorists in a crowd, how could it be abused?

_____

_____

8 Why are Disney theme parks eager to have each visitor wear a bracelet with an identifying chip?

_____

_____

F. The focus of this chapter is law and justice. New laws are created when people believe they are being treated unjustly. Based on Listening 1, choose the statement that suggests the best reason that new laws around technocreep might be created.

☐ If we continue to let technology collect personal information, it is likely that a new form of computer will someday control us all.

☐ Personal information may be freely available or even given away, but it's hard to decide when sharing benefits you.

☐ Your private information is your personal property and others using it without your permission are stealing.

Develop Your Vocabulary: "Technocreep" is a made-up compound word. A speaker using such a word will likely define it. If not, ask.

FOCUS ON GRAMMAR

Modals that Express Possibility

As you listened to the interview in Listening 1, you heard the speakers using modal auxiliaries. *Modal auxiliaries* are sometimes called "helping verbs": they work with other verbs to express ideas about time and mood. Common modals include: *shall, could, must, ought to, should* and *would*. One class of modals expresses possibility.

FUNCTIONS	MODAL	EXAMPLES	EXPLANATION
future actions, states, intentions and high possibility	will	I **will** call the police officer *in five minutes*.	It is going to happen.
general possibility, ability	can	I **can** call a police officer *anytime I want*.	It is possible to do so.
weak possibility	might	I **might** call a police officer *if I am worried*.	It is not certain you will do so, but it is a possibility.
weaker possibility or permission	may	I **may** call a police officer *if I think it is necessary*.	
weakest possibility	could	I **could** call a police officer *if there was a problem*.	

RULES	EXAMPLES
Use modals with the base form of the verb.	He **can run**. They **may run**.
Do not modify the main verb.	She **could hide**. We **will hide**.

A. Write questions using these words and modal auxiliaries.

1. will / twenty-dollar / charge

   _____

2. might / see / now / friends

   _____

3. can / computer's / privacy / help / settings

   _____

4. may / bank / someone / talk

   _____

5. could / confession / without / signed / convict

   _____

B. Write sentences on an aspect of technocreep issues around privacy. For each sentence, use a model auxiliary that illustrates the following functions.

1. future actions, states, intentions and high possibility: _____

   _____

2 general possibility, ability: _____

_____

3 weak possibility: _____

_____

4 weaker possibility or permission: _____

_____

5 weakest possibility: _____

_____

> Use what you learned about modals when you prepare assignments.

VOCABULARY BUILD 2

A. Below are words from the Academic Word List that you will find in Listening 2. Highlight the words you understand and then circle the words you use.

precedents — noun

civil
contemporary — adjectives

magistrate

verbs — compiled
constrained
expose
refined
restore

B. Fill in the blanks with the correct words to complete the paragraph.

civil	expose	refined	restore

Judges are part of the _____ service and follow its rules.

Some judges would like to _____ old punishments,

particularly the death penalty. However, opponents are quick to

_____ the unfairness of such a punishment, such as the

many innocent people falsely accused of murder. People who live in a

_____ society should not remove an innocent person's

chance for freedom.

C. Match each word to its definition.

WORDS		DEFINITIONS
❶ precedents	_____	a) restricted in some way
❷ constrained	_____	b) put together
❸ compiled	_____	c) belonging to the present time
❹ contemporary	_____	d) legal rulings that are considered during trials

D. VOCABULARY EXTENSION: Choose the word from task A that can be used to complete all of the following sentences.

1. Rudeness was not allowed and everyone was warned to be

_____.

2. His work as a _____ engineer involved the construction of roads and bridges.

3. The idea of a _____ society is to consider individuals before government and business.

4. A _____ war is when a country divides into two parties that fight.

5. We chained ourselves to the courthouse gates as an act of

_____ disobedience.

6. Refusing to treat them equally was a violation of their _____ rights.

LISTENING ❷   **Debate: *Parallel Cases from under the Pear Tree***

It is easy to forget that there are different legal systems with different views of law and justice. For example, some countries have laws that can send students to prison for cheating on exams. Ancient China had one of the earliest and longest-lasting legal systems but, at that time, studying law was not considered a noble pursuit. For this reason, a new magistrate (a position that combined detective, prosecutor and judge) relied on books describing cases to help learn the profession. Listening 2 is a debate on the magistrate system, asking whether or not that system could work today.

Before You Listen

A. A debate involves two people or two groups arguing either side of a proposition—a debatable statement. After one person presents several points, it's the duty of the other side to rebut—or reject—the points, using logical arguments as well as passionate opinions. In the end, a judge or an audience decides whose arguments have prevailed (won) and whose have failed. With a partner, think of and discuss points for and against this proposition about restoring the ancient Chinese magistrate position.

THE PROPOSITION: The modern judge, prosecutor and detective should be one person.

B. The following is an example of a traditional magistrate's creative solution to a problem. Why would such a solution be unlikely today? Discuss with a partner.

> Modern judges are mostly constrained to giving out punishments in terms of jail time, fines and community service. There is little creativity. Compare this to Chang Ch'i-hsien's solution to the problem of two heirs, each of whom complained about the division of their inherited property, claiming the other's property was better. Chang simply forced each to move to the other's house and land.

C. These words and phrases will help you understand Listening 2. Fill in the blanks with the correct words to complete the paragraph.

adversarial	innocence	recants
community service	judgments	testimony
impartially	prosecution	

The Western justice system is based on a/an _____ model in which one side, the _____, tries to show a person's guilt, while the other side, the defence, tries to demonstrate _____. During a trial, _____ is heard from witnesses before a judge _____ gives a verdict, or decision. These _____ can include fines, prison or _____, for example asking a graffiti artist to clean up others' graffiti. The legal system doesn't always work, such as when an innocent person is sent to prison until new evidence is found or a witness _____—that is, admits earlier testimony was false.

> ❶ The prosecution acts on behalf of the government.

While You Listen

D. The first time you listen, try to understand the debate arguments put forth by each side. Listen a second time and take notes. Focus on the arguments and ignore the examples. Listen a third time and decide which of the arguments are based on fact and which are based on opinion.

FOR THE PROPOSITION	AGAINST THE PROPOSITION
judges favour law over justice (opinion)	judges don't favour law over justice (opinion)
combining the roles of judge, …	
magistrates would be …	
	magistrate position …
	years …

FOR THE PROPOSITION	AGAINST THE PROPOSITION
	abuse ...
confession ...	
motivation ...	
wisdom ...	

After You Listen

E. Choose the phrase that best completes each sentence.

1 When they began their careers, Chinese magistrates _____.
   a) were already well trained
   b) had usually written a book of cases
   c) were generally unprepared

2 The case of the woman driving her car on the sidewalk is meant to show _____.
   a) a judge's creativity in giving out punishment
   b) the foolishness of people around school buses
   c) how unfair driving laws are still widely practised

3 The case of a criminal writing on top of a contract's ink stamp _____.
   a) shows the rich traditions of the Chinese magistrates
   b) points out an example of an unfit magistrate
   c) indicates the difficult crimes magistrates had to solve

4 In the case of the boat builders, the magistrate burned the boat _____.
   a) as a warning against using expensive materials
   b) as punishment for safety issues
   c) in order to count the nails being used

5 The case of the widow and the two pigs is used to explain _____.
   a) how Chinese magistrates were skilled detectives
   b) the proper ceremonies used to honour the dead
   c) how a smell led to a woman being charged with murder

F. Listening 2 ends before the two sides have an opportunity to summarize their findings. Pick one side and use your notes to write a brief summary, on a separate page, supporting your chosen side's arguments. Share your summary with a partner who has summarized the other side.

> ❗ Many discussions are informal debates and work best when facts, not opinions or emotions, are used to make decisions.

Constructing an Argument

Think of the last time you argued for something. In Chapter 7, Academic Survival Skill (page 149) you learned how to construct a thesis and give evidence to support your thesis. Once you have a thesis statement, you also need an approach—a structure for presenting your thesis and argument. An *argument* is a way of organizing ideas to guide others to a conclusion. Constructing an argument also requires understanding your audience and taking into account the time you have to speak and the venue where you will be presenting.

A. Once you have your thesis and evidence, construct your argument. Match these steps for constructing an argument to the explanations.

STEPS		EXPLANATIONS
❶ Provide a context.	_____	a) In a longer argument, briefly explain the points that you are going to discuss. In a shorter argument, simply say: *There are three points/reasons/arguments. The first one is ...* Avoid casual language, contractions and slang. Define technical terms: *Incarceration, or imprisonment/confinement, means ...*
❷ Give an overview.	_____	b) After you finish, invite the audience to ask about anything they did not understand. Use your answers to emphasize parts of your argument.
❸ Introduce your evidence.	_____	c) Use the evidence that is most likely to capture the audience's attention. Don't wait to share your best examples and ideas.
❹ Start with a prominent example.	_____	d) Explain what your thesis statement means. Most arguments are about making a change, so you may want to talk about why the current situation is unacceptable.
❺ Use signposting.	_____	e) Keep track of time and just before you are done, restate your main points and thesis. Finish by asking the audience to change their minds or take some action.
❻ Conclude with a summary and ask for change.	_____	f) Use numbers and other expressions to let your audience know where you are in your speech: *First, ..., My second point ..., Finally, ... To summarize, ... In conclusion, ...*
❼ Ask for questions.	_____	g) Relate the topic to your audience or yourself: *Today's topic relates to the tragic events that happened in our community last month ...* or *As someone whose aunt was a judge/prison guard/police officer, I know about ....*

B. Using the topic of graffiti, work with a partner and take turns practising a brief presentation for the proposition: Writing graffiti is an offence that needs to be taken more seriously. Use the steps in task A to structure your argument.

STEPS	PRESENTATION EXAMPLE
PROVIDE A CONTEXT	When I was walking here today, I passed several walls that had been covered with racist graffiti. I would like to explain how graffiti impacts victims and why graffiti offenders should be made aware of it.
GIVE AN OVERVIEW	I'd like to explain the problem of graffiti with three points.
INTRODUCE YOUR EVIDENCE	First, there are three kinds of graffiti, so-called art, tagging—which means signing something—and gang-related tags that mark out territory.
START WITH A PROMINENT EXAMPLE	In 2013, 22 percent of all San Diego graffiti was gang-related. This means …
USE SIGNPOSTING	First, gang graffiti makes younger kids think being in a gang is cool. Second, …
CONCLUDE WITH A SUMMARY AND ASK FOR CHANGE	I've explained how graffiti has financial impacts: impacts on gang membership and impacts on community feelings of safety. But those who write graffiti are only given fines and sentences. It's time for more serious consequences, for offenders to face their victims and …
ASK FOR QUESTIONS	Now, I would be happy to take any questions.

WARM-UP ASSIGNMENT
Give a Persuasive Presentation

In Focus on Speaking, you learned how to construct an argument and share it in a presentation. Now prepare a short persuasive presentation either for or against the following proposition: In a legal system, wisdom is more important than truth.

A. Use the format you learned in Focus on Speaking to organize your argument.

STEPS	NOTES
PROVIDE A CONTEXT	
GIVE AN OVERVIEW	
INTRODUCE YOUR EVIDENCE	
START WITH A PROMINENT EXAMPLE	
USE SIGNPOSTING	
CONCLUDE WITH A SUMMARY AND ASK FOR CHANGE	
ASK FOR QUESTIONS	

B. Practise your presentation with a partner. Refer to Focus on Grammar (page 160) as you discuss possibilities.

C. Present in front of the class. Ask for feedback from your teacher and classmates to see what you could improve.

VOCABULARY BUILD 3

A. Below are words and phrases from the Academic Word List that you will find in Listening 3. Highlight the words you understand and then circle the words you use.

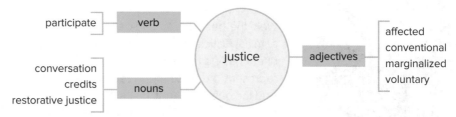

B. Highlight the word or phrase in parentheses that best completes each sentence. Key words are in bold.

❶ The focus of **restorative justice** is on the (victim / judge).

❷ Without enough **credits**, you won't (drop out of / complete) university.

❸ The prison system's **conversation** about justice is likely to be (simple / complex).

❹ Participation in the program is **voluntary** so it's not surprising some people (drop out / stay).

C. Choose the best definition for each word. Use a dictionary to check your answers.

❶ affected   a) influenced   b) willing to change something

❷ marginalized   a) comments on the side of a book   b) ignored by others

❸ participate   a) make something more difficult   b) be a part of something

❹ conventional   a) common and usual   b) uncommon and unusual

Visit My eLab to complete Vocabulary Review exercises for this chapter.

LISTENING ❸   Restoring Harmony after Murder

Imagine going home and finding your door kicked in and many of your favourite possessions broken or stolen. A few weeks later, the thief is caught, charged by police and sentenced by the court to a period in jail. Would that be enough to make you feel better about your loss? How about other, more serious crimes? For many, the answer is "no," and leads to a consideration of restorative justice as a means of connecting victims and criminal offenders. In Listening 3, Brenda Morrison talks about how restorative justice can help give victims what they need to understand, heal and move on.

Before You Listen

A. With a partner, reflect on a situation of a break-in and theft and imagine the victim and the offender have a chance to meet after the offender has been released from prison. Think of questions that might be asked. Then, role-play a conversation between the victim and offender.

B. Read this excerpt from Listening 3. In it, Brenda Morrison talks about the fact that although offenders can be punished, victims may want something else, such as a better understanding of why the offences occurred. Then, imagine teenagers are caught spraying racist graffiti in your neighbourhood on cars and homes. What would you want to say to them after they were caught? Discuss in a group.

> Well, the best way to think about restorative justice is in contrast to what our criminal justice process offers. It's a contest between the State and the alleged offender. And the people involved in that conversation are the State, those who represent the State, and the offender, and those who represent the offender. And the questions that they ask are: "What law's been broken? Who did it? What do they deserve?" That's the conversation, and in that process victims are often marginalized. Communities are marginalized, and those are the groups that are most affected by crime in our communities.

C. These words will help you understand Listening 3. Use the context to write a definition for each word in bold.

1 In terms of **accountability**, she was responsible for ensuring each case was finished.

_____

2 The **alleged** offender was released when he proved he didn't commit the crime.

_____

3 In **ascertaining** the truth, the police officer asked several witnesses for the facts.

_____

4 Adding more water to the tea was a way to **dilute** the flavour.

_____

5 It was important for his arm to **heal** after it had been broken.

_____

6 It's not a choice, but rather an **obligation** to obey the law.

_____

While You Listen

D. The first time you listen, try to understand the general idea of Morrison's concept of restorative justice. Listen a second time and indicate which of Morrison's statements are fact and which are opinion (including valid opinion). If you are unsure, refer to Focus on Listening on page 154. Listen a third time to check your answers.

FACT		STATEMENTS	OPINION
☐	❶	Traditional justice is a contest between the State and the alleged offender.	☐
☐	❷	The people involved in a conversation are the State, those who represent the State, the offender and those who represent the offender.	☐
☐	❸	In the traditional system, victims and communities are marginalized.	☐
☐	❹	The people that participate in a restorative justice process are those most affected.	☐
☐	❺	A state-based justice system focuses on the past.	☐
☐	❻	Restorative justice focuses on the future.	☐
☐	❼	What victims want to know is why? And a lot of those questions aren't answered in the criminal justice process.	☐
☐	❽	Restorative justice is very important to healing.	☐
☐	❾	To become a trainer in restorative justice, there's a lot of different training programs.	☐
☐	❿	Simon Fraser University offers some of the most comprehensive training in restorative justice, internationally.	☐

After You Listen

E. Indicate whether these statements are true or false, according to the listening.

STATEMENTS		TRUE	FALSE
❶	Morrison is Director of the Centre for Restorative Justice at the School of Criminology at Simon Fraser University.	☐	☐
❷	Morrison says restorative justice invites judges to be part of the conversation.	☐	☐
❸	Morrison says that restorative justice allows the offender to step up for direct accountability.	☐	☐
❹	Morrison denies that the aim of restorative justice is to prevent certain harms from happening again.	☐	☐
❺	The aim of all offenders in restorative justice is to seek forgiveness.	☐	☐
❻	Victims and offenders tend to meet before any contact with a facilitator.	☐	☐
❼	University training in restorative justice is available at many levels.	☐	☐

F. Answer these questions. Then, discuss in a group.

❶ Why might offenders' families and communities be part of the restorative justice conversation?

_____

_____

❷ In what ways might restorative justice look to the future instead of the past?

_____

_____

③ Which crime is Morrison talking about when she says the following?

"... sometimes people enter the process and all they want to know is the last words that loved ones said: 'What happened in the last moments? Can you tell me a little bit of this?'"

_____

_____

Academic
Survival Skill

Debating Strategies

In Focus on Speaking (page 165), you learned how to construct an argument in a presentation. But winning an argument requires using strategies that will convince both your opponent and other listeners. You also need to identify weaknesses in others' arguments.

The most important thing in a debate is to remain polite. Being rude will not impress your opponent or the audience. Attack the arguments instead of attacking the character of those giving the arguments (e.g., suggesting they are foolish). Attacking a debater's character is so common, it has a name —*ad hominum,* which is Latin for *argument to the person*. Recognizing this and other common logical fallacies (thinking errors) is an easy way to dismiss your opponents' arguments. In this case, you can say: "My opponents may wish to attack me, but it is only because they are unable to attack my arguments."

> ❶ There are dozens of common logical fallacies. Look for others online.

A. Read the following logical fallacies and examples and explain why each example argument might be false.

LOGICAL FALLACIES AND EXPLANATIONS	EXAMPLE ARGUMENTS
❶ Appeal to authority arguments are based on the ideas of a respected person or source. Challenge the qualifications of the source to point out that the ideas are not current or applicable to the thesis.	Albert Einstein said that peace cannot be kept by force; it can only be kept by understanding. _____ _____
❷ Slippery slope arguments suggest one thing will lead to more serious things. Challenge the basic assumptions and suggest the serious consequences are unrelated.	Shoplifting has to be treated seriously before offenders grow up to be murderers. _____ _____
❸ False dichotomy arguments suggest that there are only two choices. Challenge by pointing out that there are almost always other choices.	Either you get a job now or you'll be unemployed for the rest of your life. _____ _____
❹ Ad populum arguments suggest that the majority is always right. Challenge by pointing out examples of when the majority has been wrong.	Prison sentences are too short. At least 67 percent of people agree. _____ _____

FINAL ASSIGNMENT

Participate in a Debate

Use everything you learned in this chapter to participate in a debate related to justice.

A. Form a group of six. Choose a criminal offence that has been committed as your topic for debate. You can select one from a recent news story or an older crime. Each group will present their debate in front of the class.

B. Ask your teacher for approval of your choice of topic.

C. Write your topic as a proposition. Relate it to restorative justice. Three group members will argue for the proposition and three will argue against it.

THE PROPOSITION: Restorative justice is a better approach than traditional justice for the crime of ….

D. Do your research. Use the library and the Internet to find out more about the crime, restorative justice and traditional justice.

E. Plan your debate. Use this format to organize the debate and write your notes on separate pages. Construct your arguments based on what you learned in Focus on Speaking (page 165). Use modal auxiliaries to express possibility (see Focus on Grammar, page 160).

IN FAVOUR OF THE PROPOSITION	AGAINST THE PROPOSITION
❶ State the proposition and define what it means. Present three points in favour.	❷ Rebut the other team's points; this may include their interpretation of the proposition. Present three points against.
❸ Rebut the other team's points and add new points.	❹ Rebut the other team's points and add new points.
❺ Summarize your points and objections to the other teams' points and explain why your team's points have helped the proposition prevail (i.e., succeed).	❻ Summarize your points and objections to the other teams' points and explain why your team's points have made the proposition fail.

F. Review the debate format used in Listening 2 to maintain a formal and persuasive tone. Agree on the amount of time each of your team members has to speak.

G. Conduct your debate. As you participate, use what you learned in Focus on Listening (page 154) to separate opponents' facts from opinions and try to spot logical fallacies (review Academic Survival Skill, page 170).

H. After your debate, vote on which side had the more effective arguments—for or against the proposition. Once all groups have presented, ask your teacher and classmates for advice on how you might improve your presentation's content and style.

How confident are you?

Think about what you learned in this chapter. Use the table to decide what you should review.

I LEARNED ...	I AM CONFIDENT	I NEED TO REVIEW
vocabulary related to law and justice;	☐	☐
to distinguish fact from opinion;	☐	☐
about modals that express possibility;	☐	☐
how to construct an argument;	☐	☐
how to give a persuasive presentation;	☐	☐
debate strategies;	☐	☐
how to participate in a debate.	☐	☐

VOCABULARY
Challenge

Think about the vocabulary and ideas in this chapter. Use these words to write two sentences about finding justice.

contemporary	indicate	link	marginalized	restore	voluntary

_____

_____

_____

_____

_____

My eLab
Visit My eLab to build on what you learned.

© ERPI • Reproduction prohibited

APPENDIX 1
Conversation Gambits

Gambits are commonly understood ways of starting, maintaining and closing informal and formal conversations in polite ways. Practise the following on your own and with a partner.

GAMBITS	INFORMAL	FORMAL
OFFER GREETINGS	Hi. How are you?	Hello. How are you?
INTRODUCE A TOPIC	I'd like to talk to you about …	If you have a moment, I would like to discuss …
EXPLAIN A POINT	Let me explain. Here's the idea. What do you think about …?	Let me suggest … The basic idea is … The important part of the idea is …
CHECK FOR COMPREHENSION	Do you get what I'm saying? Do you follow what I've said so far?	Can I ask if you understand my point? Is everything clear so far?
SHOW YOU ARE LISTENING	[frown, nod] Really? Right. Uh-huh. OK.	[frown, nod] Yes. Are you sure?
SHOW AGREEMENT	Yes. I agree. I can't argue with that.	Yes. I agree. That's true. You've made a good point.
INTERRUPT	I'm sorry, … Excuse me, … Pardon me, but … Can I ask a question? Can I add something here?	Sorry for interrupting, but … If I can just interrupt for a moment, … If I could stop you there for a second, …
ASK THE SPEAKER TO REPEAT	Can you say that again? Could you repeat that? What was that? Excuse me? Sorry, what?	I'm not sure I follow. Would you mind repeating that? Pardon me, what did you say?
REFUSE INTERRUPTIONS	Please, let me finish. Can I just finish my point?	Perhaps if you could let me finish. May I just finish my point?
CONTINUE AFTER AN INTERRUPTION	As I was saying, … Let's see, where was I?	To get back to what I was saying, …
DISAGREE POLITELY	That's not true/right, is it? I'd say/think something different …	I'm not sure I agree. I can't say that that's a convincing point/argument.
MAKE A QUALIFICATION	That's not totally what I meant.	Although I agree with …, I also believe …
EXPRESS AN OPINION	In my opinion, … What I think … As I see it, …	My personal opinion is that …
CLARIFY THE SPEAKER'S POINTS BY RESTATING	So, what you mean is … So, what you're trying to say is …	If I can restate, first you state … Then, I understand your point is …
CLARIFY YOUR POINTS BY RESTATING	What I'm trying to say is … What I mean is …	To put it another way, … Let me explain it another way …
SUMMARIZE	All in all, what I'm trying to say is … The main points are …	To summarize, … To bring this all together, …
CLOSE THE CONVERSATION	I have to go now, but it's been great talking with you. Thanks for the chance to talk.	I'm glad we had a chance to talk. Thank you for taking the time to speak with me.

APPENDIX 2
Strategies for Improving Listening and Speaking Skills

1 Listening is made up of understanding the sounds and meanings of words as well as the pronunciation patterns of words, phrases and sentences. **In your spare time, take the opportunity to listen to podcasts in your field of study as well as recordings of short stories and novels.** Listen several times, first to get the gist and the general patterns of pronunciation, then to understand new vocabulary in context. While you listen, try pronouncing portions of what you are hearing.

2 When you listen, you acquire new vocabulary, new ideas and new ways of saying things. Research shows that simply listening to a lecture will lead to limited acquisition. Instead, you need to activate what you have heard by taking notes, reviewing them and trying to use the language in other contexts, such as in a discussion with a study partner. The most effective way of learning new ideas is to teach. **Take what you've heard in a lecture, organize it and share it with another person.** In this way, you are more likely to remember new words, expressions and ideas.

3 **Whenever you listen, remind yourself of your purpose.** In some cases, you may listen passively, not bothering to remember most of the information you hear. For example, if you are in an airport, you will hear hundreds of announcements but only need to worry about those related to your flight. In other cases, you need to listen actively, measuring each idea you hear in terms of what it means to you. You might listen to understand, to summarize, to make a decision or for other purposes. Knowing the purpose helps you focus on what to listen for.

4 **Interrupting is a key part of listening.** When you are in a conversation, one of the simplest and most basic ways to interrupt is to appear confused or frown. The other speaker will often take this as a cue to pause and explain in greater detail. Otherwise, stop the other speaker and politely ask for clarification. The speaker may repeat what was said, paraphrase the idea, provide an explanation or provide an example. If the clarification satisfies you, smile and nod. If not, ask questions to help you better understand.

5 **Listening strategies include top down and bottom up approaches.** In a *top down* approach, you listen to predict what the talk will be about (based on your background knowledge), to identify the main idea, to draw inferences (guesses based on the facts) and to summarize ideas. In a bottom up approach, you tend to listen for specific information, such as key words, directions or instructions. In bottom up listening, the main idea is not as important and you can't necessarily summarize the ideas effectively. Understanding why you are listening helps you choose between top down and bottom up approaches.

6. When you speak, you often end up repeating certain questions, answers and statements. For example, you may ask questions when you meet someone new, provide answers about yourself and make statements about everything from the weather to the latest news. For both informal and formal situations, practise these conversations in your head and say them out loud, adding details that help make you seem friendlier. **Find opportunities to speak.** For example, try engaging in short conversations with other commuters or people where you study or work.

7. You might not speak as much as you would like to because you become nervous in classroom conversations or social situations where you have to speak in front of a group of people. In these situations, you might feel that you cannot express yourself properly, perhaps because you cannot grasp the right words or keep up with what others are saying. But it's better to try and sometimes fail than to avoid speaking more than necessary. **Practising speaking is the principal way to improve your speaking skills.**

8. **In academic situations where you need to make a presentation in front of a class, spend as much time as possible on preparation, rehearsing what you have to say until it feels conversational.** Don't memorize it but speak as though you are explaining the ideas in a relaxed way to a close friend for the first time. Use confident body language and maintain eye contact with at least three people: one on either side of the room and one in the middle. This gives the impression that you're looking at everyone. Smile; smiling will help to relax both you and your audience.

9. **During classes and lectures, ask permission to record part of what you hear on your mobile phone or other audio device.** After class, listen to portions and improve your speaking skills by taking time to repeat what you have heard several times. This helps you with intonation patterns and the pronunciation of key words and expressions related to your teacher's ideas. This not only prepares you to discuss the ideas in class, but also serves as an effective study aid.

10. **When you are tested on speaking, it is often done as an interview in which you must also understand the questions you hear.** The most important thing is to ensure that you understand the question or speaking prompt. If you are not sure, politely ask for clarification. Take a moment to consider your answer and then focus on giving a complete answer. Don't try to say as little as possible to avoid making mistakes. If, part way through your answer you realize you have misunderstood the question, ask for the chance to begin again. This is better than delivering an incomplete or wrong answer.

To really improve your English, take every opportunity to read, write, speak and listen.

PHOTO CREDITS

CORBIS

Cover, p. iii © XiXinXing.

ISTOCKPHOTO

pp. viii, 66, 87 © Andrew Rich/Rich Vintage Photography.

SHUTTERSTOCK

pp. viii, 2, 23 © alphaspirit; pp. viii, 44, 65 © jaboo2foto; pp. viii, 88, 109 © design36; pp. ix, 110, 129 © Syda Productions; pp. ix, 130, 151 © Ollyy; pp. ix, 152, 172 © imagedb.com; p. 5 © Andrey_Popov; p. 14 © Georgios Kollidas; p. 18 © Andresr; p. 22 © Muh; p. 28 © Mila Supinskaya; p. 30 © NikoNomad; p. 33 © Mariday; p. 36 © Andrey Bayda; p. 47 © Rafal Olkis; p. 48 © Syda Productions; p. 49 © sigur; p. 51 © Pavel L Photo and Video; p. 52 © HUANSHENG XU; p. 55 © Chesky; p. 59 © Africa Studio; p. 60 © Kiev.Victor; p. 63 © Laborant; p. 64 © Cora Mueller; p. 70 (t) © Naeblys; p. 71 (t) © SergiyN; p. 71 (b) © Aaron Amat; p. 75 (t) © Andrey Arkusha; p. 75 (b) © Rawpixel; p. 81 © Everett Historical; p. 83 © SusaZoom; p. 89 © doomu; p. 91 © wavebreakmedia; p. 92 (l) © Vereshchagin Dmitry; p. 92 (l, c) © AleksandarMilutinovic; p. 92 (c) © Vitaliy Krasovskiy; p. 92 (r, c) © Levent Konuk; p. 92 (r) © Ribah; p. 97 © MO_SES Premium; p. 104 (t) © wellphoto; p. 104 (b) © hopsalka; p. 105 © Stokkete; p. 111 © Irina Mir; p. 112 © PhilTragen; p. 116 © Brues; p. 120 (t) © FloridaStock; p. 120 (l, c) © gualtiero boffi; p. 120 (r, c) © sommai damrongpanich; p. 120 (b) © cynoclub; p. 121 (t) © Pakhnyushchy; p. 121 (c) © tea maeklong; p. 121 (b) © Eric Isselée; p. 124 © vitstudio; p. 127 © Blend Images; p. 128 © AlexandreNunes; p. 131 © Marzolino; p. 133 © 1000 Words; p. 137 © Marharyta Kovalenko; p. 140 © PathDoc; p. 145 © Arina P Habich; p. 153 © Olga Rosi; p. 156 © Brian A Jackson; p. 157 © VGstocksudio; p. 160 © John Roman Images; p. 161 © Volt Collection; p. 162 © claudio zaccherini; p. 164 © Chinaview; p. 168 © Kzenon; p. 171 © Andresr.

THINKSTOCK

pp. viii, 24, 43 © Robert Churchill; p. 4 © oaltindag; p. 7 © zimmytws; p. 10 © ildogesto; p. 11 © Fuse; p. 12 © Wavebreakmedia Ltd; p. 17 © goldy; p. 21 © sumnersgraphicsinc; p. 26 © XiXinXing; p. 27 © George Doyle; p. 32 © Jupiterimages; p. 35 © Anthony Brown; p. 38 © 2nix; p. 40 © IPGGutenbergUKLtd; p. 42 © simonkr; p. 53 © Tijana87; p. 56 © Blaj Gabriel; p. 62 © betyarlaca; p. 68 © Goodluz; p. 70 (b) © macrovector; p. 72 © sjallenphotography; p. 73 © Paul Vasarhelyi; p. 79 © XiXinXing; p. 82 © Photos.com; p. 84 © webguzs; p. 86 © Fuse; p. 94 © 1971yes; p. 96 © ilfede; p. 98 © Vadim Volkov; p. 107 © koya79; p. 108 © Monkey Business Images; p. 114 © dolgachov; p. 118 © piccaya; p. 119 © Chromatika Multimedia; p. 120 (l, c) © Eric Isselée; p. 120 (r, c) © specnaz-s; p. 134 © jacquesvandinteren; p. 135 © Ingram Publishing; p. 141 © omgimages; p. 142 © Ingram Publishing; p. 146 © Jupiterimages; p. 147 © Antonio_Sanchez; p. 150 © AmmentorpDK; p. 155 © Jupiterimages; p. 159 © ra2studio; p. 163 © montiannoowong; p. 165 © Juergen Reinsch.